THE HAND OF POETRY

THE HAND OF POETRY

FIVE MYSTIC POETS OF PERSIA

Translations from the Poems of
Sanai, Attar, Rumi, Saadi and Hafiz
by
Coleman Barks

Lectures on Persian Poetry
by
Inayat Khan

OMEGA PUBLICATIONS
New Lebanon

The publisher wishes to thank all of the many persons who have assisted in bringing this project into printed form: Majida Gibson at Glorious Words for design of the text, not to mention the friendship and unconditional support; Barkat Curtin for executing the cover design; Firozia Joan Peebles and David Thwaite for proofreading; Alice McMullin, Jane Steinberg and Eric Woodward for financial support; Sharif Graham for the original idea; Coleman Barks for suggesting the title; and the Metropolitan Museum of Art for granting permission to use *Dancing Dervishes*, a Persian miniature from a 15th century Diwan of Hafiz.

OMEGA PUBLICATIONS INC
RD 1 BOX 1030E
NEW LEBANON, NY 12125-9801

Printed in the United States of America.
ISBN 0-930872-47-9

10 9 8 7 6 5 4 3 2 1

Table of Contents

Inayat Khan on
RUMI: Birdsong Moving Through Us
Like Rain   63

INTRODUCTION

This book, *The Hand of Poetry*, offers entrance into a
world of beauty and truth. Its method is two-fold. First
it presents five important lectures on Persian poetry
given by Pir-o-Murshid Inayat Khan, who brought
Sufism to the West. Then it offers fresh translations by
the poet Coleman Barks of some of the poetry Inayat
Khan discusses, designed to provide readers with ready
access to at least a sample of this wondrous literature,
still not easy to find in English. Thus, *The Hand of Poetry*
represents a brief, but reasonably comprehensive, intro-
duction to one of the great literatures of the world, until
recently ignored in the West.

Persian literature of the 13th century, described by a
leading authority, Professor Annemarie Schimmel, as
the "zenith" of the vast Islamic literature (she asserts it
would require a large team of scholars to master even
one branch of it), is certainly still a hidden treasure,
despite the efforts of many scholars during the last
century. Very few people in the West have learned the
language, Farsi, and the translations have often left
much to be desired in terms of their poetic appeal. This
situation is now being vigorously corrected by Coleman
Barks, our present translator, whose wonderfully lively
and poetically powerful translations of Jelaluddin Rumi
fill more than half a dozen much admired volumes, and
by other contemporary poets as well. Nevertheless, the
vast majority of classical Persian poems exist only in
manuscript, never having been printed even in the origi-
nal language! Even the lives of most of these poets do
not appear in standard encyclopedias, so the translator
has helpfully added brief accounts of what little is
known about them.

Inayat Khan was reared in a highly artistic, mainly musical household in Baroda, Gujerat, India in the 1880s and '90s. One of the household languages was Urdu, an Indian adaptation of Farsi, and he took a special interest in poetry already in early youth. The poetry he discusses here was known to him for virtually his whole life, and it came as something of a shock when he came to the West in 1910 to discover that very few people had even heard of these great poets. When he spoke about them, he spoke (as always) entirely *ex tempore*, never using any notes as far as we know. His work in presenting these poets was, as in many other areas, pioneering work. Omar Khayyam was the only one of these poets well-known to Western audiences, largely because of Edward Fitzgerald's translation of the *Rubaiyat*, considered today of dubious value as a translation.

Now, seventy years later, this poetry has become much better known in the West, yet it is still possible to ask a literature professor if she has heard of Jelaluddin Rumi and receive a negative answer. Therefore, it is highly *apropos* to continue Inayat Khan's pioneering effort by this new presentation of his teachings and the work of the poets themselves.

This book also represents a significant step forward in the presentation of the texts of Inayat Khan. This is the first time his lectures have been presented in a book for the public in words as close as possible to the actual words he spoke. This has been made possible by the scholarly series, *The Complete Works of Hazrat Pir-o-Murshid Inayat Khan* (East-West, The Hague, 1988-). The second volume of that series (*1923 I*, published in 1989), includes these five lectures. *The Complete Works* provides a text of each lecture based on the earliest and best manuscript, most often a shorthand record. In the case of these lectures, however, no shorthand record has survived (Inayat Khan's secretaries were not travelling with him), and our basic manuscript is typewritten. We do not know who took down the lecture or prepared the typescript, which is slightly edited; it may well have been Rabia Martin, the leader of the Sufi Center in San Francisco. Because *The Complete Works* is restricted in circulation, the present publication makes widely available for the first time Inayat Khan's actual words.

The lecture series represented here took place on Tuesday afternoons at 2:30 p.m. from April 3rd to May 8th, 1923, in the gallery of the Paul Elder Bookstore, the leading such institution in the San Francisco of that day. Inayat Khan was billed as "A Pilgrim of Music, Literature and Philosophy," and he gave two other series, one on music and the other on spiritual philosophy, on Wednesday mornings and Thursday evenings respectively. Miss Hayat Stadlinger, still a resident of Oakland, California, vividly recalls attending these lectures as a young woman. She recalls that Inayat Khan sat in the vestibule and warmly greeted each person coming in, with a display of white calla lilies at his feet. She also recalls that the audience was quite large and enthusiastic. A payment of one dollar was required (not inexpensive in those days), and the Gallery, located at 239 Post Street, was proudly declared to be "air conditioned and vitalized by electro-ozone equipment" (perhaps this will give pause to those who imagine that the New Age movement began in the 'sixties). Unfortunately, the text of one lecture, the second in the series, on Omar Khayyam, appears not to have been preserved. The beautifully prepared brochure gives an unmistakable flavor of the times, and so we reproduce the page referring to the present series.

SUFI POETS: A series of six Tuesday afternoon lectures, April 3rd to May 8th, inclusive

---

Tuesday Afternoon, April 3rd, at 2:30 o'clock
THE POET AND THE PROPHET.

The various scriptures of the nations are interpreted by the Prophets and Spiritual Poets of every age, not as dogmas, but as appeals to the heart of man. They point the way to our spiritual freedom; with one stroke of the pen they emancipate us as souls, and with the other they have shown us to speak straight from the heart, and with all spontaneity, breaking the barriers of human limitation and spiritual bondages. To interpret Persian religious and philosophic poetry with full understanding of the sense intended by the writer, requires intimate acquaintance with Moslem thought, and in particular with theology and mysticism.

Tuesday Afternoon, April 10th, at 2:30 o'clock
OMAR KHAYYAM.

All authorities, intellectual and spiritual (despite the fallacies of modern interpretations), describe this poet as one who drank deeply of wisdom, and this is revealed through his many famous works on astronomy, mathematics, metaphysics and philosophy. He was a master of the exact sciences.

Tuesday Afternoon, April 17th, at 2:30 o'clock
JALLAL-U-DIN-RUMI.

The Masnavi has all the beauty of the Psalms, the music of the hills, the color and scent of roses; but it has more than that, it expresses in song the yearnings of the soul to be reunited with God.

Tuesday Afternoon, April 24th, at 2:30 o'clock
SHAIKH MUSLIH-UD-DIN SAADI.

The Gulistan (Rose Garden) represents the consummation of a wide knowledge of life and men, and though Saadi's own life was fraught with hardships and trials, he maintained serenity of spirit and a heart attuned to the great problems of humanity. In the simplicity of his heart he says tenderly of his own work:

> "We give advice in its proper place,
> Spending a lifetime in the task.
> If it should not touch any one's ear of desire,
> The messenger told his tale;
> It is enough."

Tuesday Afternoon, May 1st, at 2:30 o'clock
HAFIZ.

Hafiz breathes originality in all his works; he has defects, but only his own; he has beauties, but only his own. He may be condemned, but cannot be compared. He is considered by some authorities to be the greatest poet of any age or country. The name Hafiz literally means "the man who remembers." He spent his life remembering God and preserved these remembrances in verses which to this day are consulted as oracles.

Tuesday Afternoon, May 8th, at 2:30 o'clock
FARID-DU-DIN ATTAR.

The Mantiqu't Tayr is a description of the Mystical Quest of the Birds (Sufi Pilgrims) for the Simurgh (God).

1st. Valley of Search.
2nd. Valley of Love.
3rd. Valley of Knowledge.
4th. Valley of Non-attachment.
5th. Valley of Unity.
6th. Valley of Amazement.
7th. Valley of Realization of God.

Tickets: Single lecture, One Dollar

Season Ticket, six lectures, Five Dollars

I would like to end on a personal note. I am one of the editors (along with Munira van Voorst van Beest, now deceased) of *The Complete Works*, and after the publication of the volume *1923 I* in 1989, I suggested to my dear friend and colleague, Abi'l-Khayr of Omega Publications, that we put out a volume of these lectures along with appropriate passages from the poets discussed. I only planted this seed; Abi'l-Khayr germinated it, cultivated it, and it grew into the garden into which you are about to step. I cannot possibly express the joy I feel at this undreamed-of outcome.

Sharif Graham
Tucson, Arizona
March 14, 1993

Translator's Preface

There's a story of how wisdom was once collected in one place like a huge pond of mercury, then shattered into tiny bits, widely dispersed over the planet. But every so often some of the fragments roll together, not to re-form the pond, but as clusters to remind us of what the wholeness once was.

Such groupings occurred among the Hassids of Poland and Russia in the 17th and 18th centuries, in the Greece of the pre-Socratics, in the early 17th century in England, in Paris during the 1870's, and for twenty years in the middle of the last century in the northeastern United States. These gorgeous rock-hollow pools *do* occur. One of the most brilliant was in the Middle East, among Persian-speakers of the 12th, 13th, and 14th centuries. Attar, Sanai, Rumi, Saadi, and Hafiz—an illustrious group that serves as the jeweled crown of world literature. Nothing quite like them has re-appeared, anywhere.

They were artists and also great soul-shepherds. They were dervish poets, that mysterious and yet profoundly simple heart-line that goes back before Abraham to ancient Egypt, and into the pre-dawn of consciousness. When I first saw one of those fourteen thousand year old "high-five" hand-drawings in a cave in southern France, I felt the Friendship at the deep core that sufis, and poets, offer. They work with words, only one of their crafts, to let beauty come in, the admiration for which is at the center of any religious impulse. Here is what Hazrat Inayat Khan says about that:

> Whatever differences in principles of what is right and wrong the various religious faiths may show, no two individuals will ever differ in this one

natural principle: that every soul seeks after beauty, and that every virtue, righteousness, good action, is nothing but a glimpse of beauty. When once he or she has made this moral one's own, that person does not need to follow a particular belief or faith or restrict oneself to a particular path. He or she can follow the Hindu way, the Muslim way, the way of any church or faith, provided one treads this royal road: that the whole universe is but an immanence of beauty. We are born with the tendency to admire it in every form, and we should not blind ourselves by being dependent on one particular line of beauty. (p.208, *The Art of Being and Becoming*)

****

But why are these bits and pools of mercury so elusive and so seldom come upon? The intricate balance of verbal artistry and revelation is rare, it seems to me, because eloquence connects deeply with the shadow-side, with material desires, the *nafs*, and with the ego. What language does so spectacularly is lie, that silver-tongued projector of illusions. The combination of a master of language with a master of light makes for a dicey dance. Rumi keeps reminding us how words obscure and deceive. All they can say about God is something like, "He is not a weaver." Not much direct truth there, and yet, "Those who love words must use them to get to God." Words flirt. They tease and imitate and come close, but they are not the experience they point to. Silence, friendship, and perhaps music, live nearer the reality.

Rumi again:

Listen to presences inside poems.
Let them take you where they will.

Translation, when and if it ever happens, tries to get out of the way and let a taste of these great presences through. They're called True Human Beings in the sufi tradition. They have been, and are, here with us. This work hopes to be part of that community.

Let the beauty we love be what we do.

RUMI

Coleman Barks
August 31, 1992

THE POET AND THE PROPHET

THE POET AND THE PROPHET

*B*eloved ones of God,

My subject for today is "The Poet and the Prophet." In the English language there is a saying in which always the name of "prophet" is connected with that of "poet," although "prophet" denotes much more than the meaning sometimes attributed to this word in the West. The reason is that very often the word "prophet" is used for someone who tells the future, who makes prophecy, but in point of fact the field of the prophet is much larger than making prophecies only. The word "Prophet" includes Master, Saint, Seer, Mystic and Teacher.

The source of poetry and of the prophetic gift is no doubt one and the same: poetry receives its inspiration from the same source as prophecy only if the poet is a real poet. Nevertheless, a poet is not necessarily a prophet, but a Prophet is certainly a poet.

The reason for this you see illustrated in the mythology of the Hindus by Sarasvati, the Goddess of music and literature. Her ornaments, her sitting with the peacock,

with the vina, holding in one hand the cards, in the
other a lotus flower—all this means that a true knowl-
edge of divine wisdom expresses itself in the realm of
beauty, the beauty of tone and rhythm in music.

And what is poetry? It is half music. It is the music of
ideas. It has sharp and flat notes as in music. It has
different modes. Its rhythm represents music. Divine
inspiration always expresses itself in beautiful form; it is
never without beauty. This explains to us that all that is
beautiful is a divine expression; the more beautiful it is,
the greater it is in divine essence.

No doubt in receiving the inspiration of poetry, action is
necessary from both sides—from the side of the poet,
and from the divine spirit. A poet who brings his heart
to a condition which allows him to, so to speak, swim in
the ocean of divine wisdom will naturally move his
arms in rhythm. It is not that he expresses poetry in
rhythm, but he receives knowledge in rhythm. The
rhythm he receives is the only rhythm; the music he
hears in life, he expresses in words, according to the
knowledge of language he possesses.

There is a wonderful example of this in a Hindu poet of
long ago. He was a man of very humble origin, the son
of a cotton weaver; a man who in childhood received no
education. All the education he had was from life, what
life taught him; and his life became his rhythm, and was
so harmonious that the Brahmans of that day, who
never allowed the other castes to come near, invited
him to a dinner party.

A feast of the Brahmans has a peculiar way in which it
is arranged. Everyone has his own board on which he
sits, and the dinner is served on leaves. The poet was
no doubt honored by their invitation, but his board was
not placed in the same row with the Brahmans. He

3

noticed this, but his rhythm was not changed; he accepted.

And there comes a kind of entertainment during the dinner, when each one has a chance of expressing himself by reciting or singing. This shows what they like, what they fancy, what they are—to what key their soul is tuned. And when it came the turn of the poet to say something, he said a verse which he had made then and there. It is a beautiful verse, but its meaning is that, "thanks be to the Creator who has brought me into an insignificant family, that has made me greet all, high or low, whatever they may be. If I were born in a high caste, probably I would have been dead, as many proud ones have died, of conceit."

The Brahmans were embarrassed, and they saw the truth of the philosophy. It was beautiful, and no thoughtful person could deny the beauty that lies in recognizing the divine in man, regardless of his rank or birth. And it was said on the occasion when the feast was given, "The one who knows Brahma, he is Brahman." In other words, the one who sees God, the one who recognizes God in all, is a Brahman.

The wonderful book of verses that this Indian poet wrote was held for centuries as a scripture; it is still regarded as a scripture, and there is a great following of this particular creed or philosophy. And the language of this man is very ordinary; so you may wonder that his poetry would be accepted in a country rich in languages, as India is with its Sanskrit, Hindustani, and sixty different dialects. There must be some reason for it. The reason is that, inside, it was all literature. Within the outer cover was the true inner form. It was a living beauty.

Writing poetry by making an effort is like doing any

other labor. It is a mental labor. The true poet, or the poet who is linked with the Prophet, does not make any effort. It comes to him like the falling of the rain. Yes, he must express it in words, but that also becomes easy for him. It is not true that words come from the divine source, for words do not belong there, words belong here. But the words come so easily, one cannot help but think that they come from the divine source.

What in reality comes from the divine source is that light in which nothing is closed to the eyes of the mind. The mind begins to see. The mind of the inspired soul differs in this way from the ordinary mind. The ordinary mind is in a room where there is everything, but no light. He cannot find the things that are there; he cannot touch anything or see anything.

The inspired mind is able to touch everything that is there. Therefore as ideas become revealed to the heart of the inspired, so words and verses come to him. The language stands out as if it were revealed, but it is only the light. When the light has fallen, all is clear and he has only to select for himself.

So, for the inspired poet it is not at all difficult to express. It is all there. You may ask, "Where does the light fall? What becomes clear?" It is his own world. All that he has learned, all that he has heard and acquired—that is his world. And when that light has fallen, the dark room is light. All that he could not see before has become plain to him. It is wonderful.

In the life of many inspired people we read that the door of their inspiration was opened from the moment that they loved someone in this world. Poetry began in their life from the time that love sprang out of the heart. What a beautiful and wonderful conception! But if there is any divine element, it is in the heart of man.

And when the heart of man has opened, the divine element rises and manifests to the world. How true it is: the rhythm of life dies when love is done. It seems as if the rhythm of life is gone when the heart has become cold.

There are other instances when a person has gone through a great deal of pain, that poetry springs up; but only if pain has melted the heart, not if the heart is frozen. If the heart is melted, then the nature responds. Poetry is the innate nature of man, and it comes out as the soul develops.

You do not need to be a poet in order to express it, you can express it in all things; in painting or writing, in action, in the everyday life. One's thoughtfulness, one's consideration in dealing with others, one's courtesy: it all comes as poetry in the form of manner. It is all poetry. When one remembers to say nothing that will make a dissonant chord; when one thinks to speak the word that will bring harmony and sweetness. You do not need to write, you can express your heart in a different way. The poetic spirit, the poetic gift, can be expressed in your life.

The poet who cannot express his poetry in his life is not complete. He has not reached that stage where his poetry can be called a ripened poetry. It is not what we say, it is what we are. We each express our heart, soul and condition in all we do. But the tendency of receiving all the beauty we can receive, and giving it to others —that is the poetic tendency, and this grows into the Prophetic tendency.

The great soul must express himself. Why does he do it? He does it because it is a natural human inclination that all the beautiful thoughts, the wonderful things that man sees, his first thought is to show them to one who is standing near: "Look, how wonderful." He cannot be satisfied without.

When we see in the history of the world, Solomon, David, Abraham, Moses, Zarathustra, Jesus, Mohammed, Rama, Krishna, Shiva, Buddha, all of them—they have given truth in poetry, in verse. The reason is that it makes their souls dance when they feel this, when they are conscious of being in God. It is said, "We live, move and have our being in God." If the soul became conscious of this, it would dance, it could not stand still. The dancing soul cannot express itself except in rhythm and in poetry. It cannot refrain from expressing itself in a music which appeals to other souls.

The poetry of Hafiz, of Rumi, is still, in the East, something living. After them many poets came and took up the same way of expressing themselves; but no one could strike the same note. In spiritual things there is no competition. Competition is in material things. So there have been many poets since Hafiz, but no one could strike the same note. No one could equal him.

The inspiration of Rumi was different, it was more mystical. The feeling that one has in the poetry of Rumi is different than in Hafiz. In the poetry of Hafiz there is rhythm, beauty, love; in the poetry of Rumi there is deep insight and love and recognition of the divine in all beings. Many souls in the East have arrived to the stage of saintliness by reading the inspired writings of Rumi.

And even now, many centuries after he passed, no one with tender and fine feelings can read his poems without shedding tears. It seems it has life. Behind the words there is divine light. It has an influence which can pierce through the heart, which can remind man of the true character of life. It is truth; it is nature. Rumi

presents to humanity an unveiled secret of the word of
life in the form of poetry.

The presentation of Hafiz is different, although Hafiz
has a great respect for the writings of Rumi. He says in
his remarks regarding the writings of Rumi which he
has written in Persian verse: "When I think of the great
work of Rumi, though I will not call him a prophet, yet
he has brought to the world a scripture."

Now the question is, "Are poets born? Are prophets
born?" The answer is that we are all born, born for all
that we do and have and accomplish in life. No soul in
the world is without a particular mission to perform and
accomplish, and the misery of every soul is in not hav-
ing come to the understanding of the purpose for which
he is born. The lifetime of confusion is always caused
by souls wandering all the time away from the purpose
for which they were born.

There is a great mistake man often makes: he is so ready
to take a fancy to things, and to go after his momentary
fancies, going from one thing to another, so in time he
loses the thread which makes him feel his way, his work
in life, his place, and what he was to accomplish. And
once this thread is lost, then man is away from home.
He does not find himself at home in his own country, in
his own home; take him to Paradise and he will not feel
at home because he has lost that thread. There is a song
called "Home, Sweet Home," but our true home and the
sweetest home is the place which is our place in life.

In the harp there is a place for every wire, and when
that wire is not placed right, it will not serve the pur-
pose—it will not give the sweet sound that is expected
of it. All human beings in this world are as different
strings of one instrument, the universe, on which the
Divine Being plays His music. And the power of feeling

that is given to man, is for him to seek through life his place, his purpose. And the closer he comes to his purpose, the better he feels, for his only happiness is in his purpose through life.

It is no use asking of people who tell fortunes, or of clairvoyants or spirit mediums, what one's purpose is. What right or what power has another to know one's place? It is one's own responsibility to find out.

Poetry and prophecy have their roots in every soul. There is a faculty of intuition from which poetry and prophecy both are born. Although there are differences, and great differences, between individuals—at the same time there is no individual who has not in his heart that spark which may be called divine and, if one realizes this, one will see that nothing is impossible to man. There is no attainment which is not possible for a human being. Or, if there is, the lack is on his part, not on the part of God. It is by our lack of patience, thought, stillness, power of will, action that produces harmony and peace, that we become confused through life and wander away from that cord that connects us with our purpose, with divine life, with all inspiration and knowledge, which, if one sought thoughtfully and earnestly, one could certainly find.

Yes, there are two distinct works that are the works of the poet and the prophet. The distinct work of the poet is to prepare the heart to receive that light which comes; and the work of the prophet is to bring that light and pour it into the hearts of men. This work is done by each individual in a small way. Mothers can do this for their children. Kind friends can do this for their fellow-men. They can prepare their hearts with gentleness, with living love, and they can sow in their hearts all that is necessary there to be produced.

9

But not everyone can do this, and when one who is not ripe for the work attempts it, he does more harm than good. Very often people are only anxious to make a sister, brother or friend, see from their own point of view, or act as they wish them to do, and they arouse antagonism. They only produce a kind of irritation, and the more they touch this irritation, the more it becomes sore, and the outcome is fatal. Therefore, it is not the work of everyone to do this. Before one tries, one must see if he can stand on his own feet; and then one must see how thought and influence work upon another. And the best way of teaching is by example. Words only annoy. And words without life have no power. What brings the best results is in acting one's own theory, living one's belief, practising one's idea. This makes one the example of his idea, and then he does not need to say. He is.

Those whose hearts are awakened cannot help but accept the teaching, the thought, the help that is given. But in point of fact what the great teachers have done, is that they have brought to the world a living God. In the world there is a belief in God, but where does one find the living God?

What one wants is the living God. For those who turn their backs on God, it is not for the reason that they are against God, but for the reason that they cannot find the living God. What was brought by the prophets of all times was the living God—to enlighten, to help, to strengthen humanity towards perfection.

SANAI: The Good Darkness

Translator's Introduction
Sanai: The Good Darkness

We know almost nothing about Sanai other than
that he lived in Ghazna and was attached to the court of
Bahramshah, whose reign lasted from 1118 until 1152. Sanai
probably died around 1150. His best known work is *The
Walled Garden of Truth* (1131). A collection of lyrics has also
survived.

The most famous legend about Sanai involves the cen-
tral transformation in his life from court poet to the tough
ecstatic who wrote *The Hadiqa*. The Sultan of Ghazna,
Bahramshah, was starting out on a military campaign to
India. Sanai was along to record the battles in verse and gen-
erally to celebrate Bahramshah's eminence, as court poets
were paid to do. In fact, Sanai had just completed a eulogy,
when the expedition passed a walled garden (*firdaus* in Pers-
ian, from whence our "paradise"). They heard beautiful
music and singing coming from within the enclosure. They
investigated and saw that it was the notorious Sufi mystic,
drunkard, and teacher, Lai-Khur. He saw the sultan and pro-
posed a toast, "To the blindness of Bahramshah!" Some of the
officers objected, and Lai-Khur explained, "Bahramshah is
going on this foolish expedition to India when he is needed
at home, and besides, what he is looking for is in himself."
Bahramshah recognized the truth of what the madman said,
but not enough to turn his army around. Then Lai-Khur pro-
posed another toast, "To Hakim Sanai, and his even greater
blindness!"

"What do you mean?"

"You are unaware of the purpose of your life. You will
come before the throne of God bringing these silly poems in
praise of political stupidities." Sanai looked in Lai-Khur's
eyes, and suddenly he knew his life's purpose. He quit the
service of the sultan, even though he was offered half the
wealth of the realm and the sultan's daughter in marriage.
Bahramshah was desperate, having received the same

12

darshan and been unable to act in response. But Sanai was unshakeable in his new state. To absorb the illumination, he went on hajj. When he arrived back in Ghazna from Mecca, he had with him the *Hadiqa*.

I would emphasize the toughness in Sanai. He awakens more by accusation and arrest than does Rumi. There is a Shams-like lightning here, preceding Rumi's summer thunder.

Most of the Sanai translations were done in collaboration with Major Stephenson's 1908 volume. David Pendlebury's more recent work has a deep attunement to Sanai, and the "Afterword" in his small volume is very profound and beautiful. I have not tried to "improve" any of Pendlebury's work, but I have worked with a few of the examples of Sanai's poetry that E.H. Browne translates in his *Literary History of Persia*, Vol II.

Teaching Schoolboys

You don't distinguish between
what is health and what is torture.

You can't tell the difference between
the hidden world and this one.

You are not traveling the path.
You are a boy playing,
and proud of your independence.

If the glamour of a mistress is enough
to satisfy, why do you need God?

If you *know* what delights,
how can you be drawn toward eternity?

But be sometimes flexible teaching schoolboys.
If one of them has difficulty learning
a particular lesson, be gentle.
Don't discourage any child
with harsh criticism.

Put sweet dried fruit in his lap.
Rub his head. Help him to try again.

If, though, your student refuses
to concentrate on the page,
if he won't read, send for the strap.

Threaten to take him to authorities.
Say that he will be shut up in a rat-house
and that the Head Rat will eat him!

This is how we keep moving on the way.
Little tastes encourage us.

And there are books which we must attempt
to read, the prophets. Be friendly
with those, and grow like schoolchildren
into understanding, remembering though,

that this world is full of people
who never read, and remain
in a dim, undeveloped stupor.

Streaming

When the path ignites a soul,
there's no remaining in place.

The foot touches ground,
but not for long.

The way where love tells its secret
stays always in motion,
and there is no *you* there, and no reason.

The rider urges his horse to gallop,
and so doing, throws himself
under the flying hooves.

In love-unity there's no old or new.
Everything is nothing.
God alone is.

For lovers the phenomena-veil is very transparent,
and the delicate tracings on it cannot
be explained with language.

Clouds burn off as the sun rises,
and the love-world floods with light.

But cloud-water can be obscuring,
as well as useful.

There is an affection that covers the glory,
rather than dissolving into it.

It's a subtle difference,
like the change in Persian
from the word "friendship"
to the word "work."

That happens with just a dot
above or below the third letter.

There is a seeing of the beauty
of union that doesn't actively work
for the inner conversation.

Your hands and feet must move,
as a stream streams, working
as its Self, to get to the ocean.
Then there's no more mention
of the search.

Being famous, or being a disgrace,
who's ahead or behind, these considerations
are rocks and clogged places
that slow you. Be as naked as a wheat grain
out of its husk and sleek as Adam.

Don't ask for anything other
than the presence.

Don't speak of a "you"
apart from That.

A full container cannot be more full.
Be whole, and nothing.

The Wild Rose of Praise

Those unable to grieve,
or to speak their love,
or to be grateful, those
who can't remember God
as the source of everything,

might be described as vacant wind,
or a cold anvil, or a group
of frightened old people.

Say the Name. Moisten your tongue
with praise, and be the spring ground,
waking. Let your mouth be given
its gold-yellow stamen like the wild rose's.

As you fill with wisdom,
and your heart with love,
there's no more thirst.

There's only an unselfed patience
waiting on the doorsill, a silence
which doesn't listen to advice
from people passing in the street.

Energetic Work

If you want the pearl,
leave the inland desert,
and wander by the sea.

Even if you don't find it,
at least you've been
near the water.

Be a warrior! Desire *something*
powerfully! Saddle your horse
and get ready for the quest.

Don't accept a crown
made of this visible sky.
Wait for what Gabriel brings.

Be energetic in the work
that takes you to God!

The weak and the sickly only *think*
about surrender. Lie down before
the door you long to go through.

Open your loving completely.
Only a dog sits idly
licking a bone.

The Good Darkness

There is great joy in darkness.
Deepen it.

Blushing embarrassments
in the half-light
confuse,

but a scorched, blackened, face
can laugh like an Ethiopian,
or a candled moth,
coming closer to God.

Brighter than any moon, Bilal,
Muhammed's Black Friend,
shadowed him on the night journey.

Keep your deepest secret hidden
in the dark beneath daylight's
uncovering and night's spreading veil.

Whatever's given you by those two
is for your desires. They poison,
eventually. Deeper down, where your face
gets erased, where life-water runs silently,

there's a prison with no food and drink,
and no moral instruction, that opens on a garden
where there's only God. No self,
only the creation-word, *BE.*

You, listening to me, roll up the carpet
of time and space. Step beyond,
into the one word.

In blindness, receive what I say.
Take *"There is no good...."*
for your wealth and your strength.

Let *"There is nothing...."* be
a love-wisdom in your wine.

Naked in the Bee-House

Being humble is right for you now.
Don't thrash around showing your strength.

You're naked in the bee-house!
It doesn't matter how powerful
your arms and legs are.

To God, that is more of a lie
than your weakness is.

In his doorway your prestige
and your physical energy are just dust
on your face. Be helpless
and completely poor.

And don't try to meet his eye!
That's like signing a paper
that honors yourself.

If you can take care of things, do so!
But when you're living at home with God,
you neither sew the world together
with desires nor tear it apart
with disappointments.

In that place existence itself
is illusion. All that is, is one.

Lost in that, your personal form
becomes a vast, empty mosque.

When you hold on to yourself,
you're a fire-worshipping temple.
Dissolve, and let everything get done.
When you don't, you're an untrained colt,
full of erratic loving and biting.
Loyal sometimes, then treacherous.

Be more like the servant who owns nothing
and is neither hungry nor satisfied,
who has no hopes for anything,
and no fear of anyone.

An owl living near the king's palace
is considered a bird of misfortune,
ragged and ominous. But off in the woods,
sitting alone, its feathers grow splendid
and sleek like the Phoenix restored.

Musk should not be kept near water or heat.
The dampness and the dryness spoil
its fragrance. But when the musk is at home
in the musk bladder, fire and wetness
mean nothing. In God's doorway your guilt
and your virtue don't count.

Whether you're Muslim, or Christian, or
fire-worshipper, the categories disappear.

You're seeking, and God is what is
sought, the essence beyond any cause.

External theological learning moves like a moon
and fades when the sun of experience rises.

We are here for a week, or less.
We arrive and leave almost simultaneously.

To be is not to be.

The *Qur'an* says, "They go hastening,
with the Light running on before them."

Clear the way! Muhammed says, "How fine!"
A sigh goes out, and there is union.

Forget how you came to this gate, your history.
Let that be as if it had not been.

Do you think the day plans its course

by what the rooster says?

God does not depend on any of his creatures.
Your existence or non-existence is insignificant.
Many like you have come here before.

When the fountain of light is pouring,
there's no need to urge it on!
That's like a handful of straw
trying to help the sun. "This way!
Please, let this light through!"

The sun doesn't need an announcer.
The lamp you carry is your self-reliance.
The sun is something else!

Half a sneeze might extinguish your lantern,
whereas all a winter's windiness
cannot put That out.

The road you must take has no particular name.
It's the one composed of your own sighing
and giving up. What you've been doing
is not devotion. Your hoping and worrying
are like donkeys wandering loose,
sometimes docile, or suddenly mean.

Your face looks wise at times,
and ashamed at others.

There is another way, a pure blankness
where those are one expression.

Omar once saw a group of boys on the road
challenging each other to wrestle.
They were all claiming to be champions,
but when Omar, the fierce and accomplished
warrior, came near, they scattered.

All but one, Abdullah Zubair.
Omar asked, "Why didn't you run?"

"Why should I? You are not a tyrant,
and I am not guilty."

When someone knows his own inner value,
he doesn't care about being accepted
or rejected by anyone else.

The prince here is strong and just.
Stand wondering in his presence.
There is nothing but That.

Earthworm Guidance

God knows what depth and shallows
each soul can navigate, the draught
of every creature. God creates

your wisdom as part of his wisdom,
that has no mind in it. The mind
is made of elements, just as desire

comes from the body. Another knowing
lives outside of time. Silence
before that is the greatest eloquence.

Your best life-food is a bare table.
You have no desire capable of wishing
for what God has already made for you.

Connect tomorrow with today and enter
a new joy. God speaks! That's enough!
God is searching for you! Be like

a cripple. Remain quiet, and in one place.
Ignorance is right with that intelligence.
The One who makes existence non-existent

stops the menstrual rhythm to build
a child. Your form has God's mystery
in it. God knows you much better

than you do yourself. Don't cry
your grief. God is already saying it.
He hears the ant's foot touching

the rock at night, and the stone
shifting in the stream, and the worm's
song of praise inside the ground.

As the worm receives sustenance
from the earth it moves through,
so we are given guidance.

Follow what you live within, the given,
or you'll come to the end swimming
in an ocean of your own shame.

The Puzzle

Someone who keeps aloof from suffering
is not a lover. I choose your love
above all else. As for wealth
if that comes, or goes, so be it.
Wealth and love inhabit separate worlds.

But as long as you live here inside me,
I cannot say that I'm suffering.

The Time Needed

Years are needed before the sun working on
a Yemeni rock can make a bloodstone.

Months must pass before cotton seed
can provide a seamless shroud.

Days go by before a handful of wool
becomes a halter rope.

Decades it takes a child
to change into a poet.

And civilizations fall and are ploughed under
to grow a garden on the ruins,
the true mystic.

A Soul's Journey Through the Time-Worlds
I.

Thrown down from my origin, I have been nursed
in this miserable world by a presence
embodied in the motions of the sky,

She the same who cared for Adam,
and led his children up
through the scale of consciousness
according to their capacities.

She is the whole
within which all things grow,
and the natural propagative power.

She calls to the cypress,
and it rises up straight. To man,
and her living fluid moves to make him erect.

So I was formed,
and wandered in the desert,
and through the mountains haunted
by wild animals around me and inside me.

Then a clarity woke in me, and I saw my soul's face,
and felt drawn upward, but pulled down still too,
by the other, contended for,
                              bewildered, and without
guidance, I ran, as from a burning house,
onto a narrow, upward-spiraling, path.

Dangerous cliffs, the summit far off.
My only hope was to die.

II.

Then through that dim murkiness,
I saw an old man with a radiant face.

"You are the moon!" I called out.
"Where did you come from?"

"I am beyond substance and space.
I am creation's cause, here to lead you
back to your home. Hold close,
and let my fire consume you. Don't be afraid
of losing your strength here. This fire
is one which has a spring of eternal water
inside it. As your animal-soul dies,
your new soul will be born.
Live humbly with me, and I will
raise you into majesty."

He talked more to me in silence,
without using syllables. He gave me
love and light and eyes to see,
and together we set out.

III.

The first day we came to a huge ash-heap
overrun with wolves, their jaws dripping
with foul meat. They did nothing but fight
and snarl at shadows of themselves,
wretched and inane.

And there I saw a snake, a viper with seven faces
on its single head, gulping and choking
with each breath.
                    "These are images of
your devouring nature," said my guide.
"They can kill you, unless you stay close

to the emerald that can stun and burst
the eyes of these monsters."

He turned his face toward them then,
and they saw and slunk away, scuffing
the road with their tails.

We came to another place, a valley where fiends
lived with eyes squinting from the napes of their necks,
and baboons on heavy haunches were swinging
their leaden arms aimlessly.

"These," he said, "are forms
of your meanness and greed."

"Master, who rules this region?"

"A lazy, sour king,
who never gives anyone anything."

We left, and came to a vast gulf
that seemed uncrossable.

"Go forward, with courage.
You have one beside you

who can divide the waters
like Moses. Step into the ocean."

And I did, and he became the pilot,
and I the ship. He became Jonah.
I, the fish. I carried him,
till we touched land, and my feet were dry.

"Now climb," he said,
and I stood amazed, for there was nothing
but air. "Do I do this
with my mind, or my imagination?"

"Neither. Leave those bows unstrung.
Become an arrow, and fly to the mark
with feathered feet."

And I did, and soon we rested
in a realm of light.

Cold and silvery, with a lovely
waxing and waning.

"The king's messenger,
the moon, lives here."

And farther on, I saw a green island,
and we went there, and entered the castle,
where magicians with dragon heads
and fish tails made evil appear
as good, ravens as golden birds,
and dunghills as gardens.

All sensualities looked charming there,
and alluring, as Zuleikha pictured them
for Joseph. Anger, concupiscence, and pride
were there, in beautiful guises.

"This," said my guide, "is a purging place.
Taste what's here. Swallow these poisons,
for in them there's freedom and health,
and hidden vitality and strength."

I drank them to the dregs,
and night vanished. A glad dawn
broke over the hills.

My eyes opened in paradise, looking out
on the dark blue harbor, and the azure city.

"This is the end of time.
Death cannot touch you now."

ATTAR: Street Sweeper

FARIDUDDIN ATTAR

B*eloved ones of God,*

I wish to address today the subject of Attar, and of his work. Fariduddin Attar is one of the most ancient poets of Persia, and it is no exaggeration to say that the work of Attar has been the inspiration of Rumi and of many spiritual souls and many poets of Persia. He has pointed out the way to the ultimate aim of life, by making a sort of picture in a poetic form. Almost all the great teachers of the world, if ever they have been able to show the right way to seeking souls, always have had to adopt a symbolical form of expression in the form of the story or legend that might give the key to one who is ready to know, and might interest the one who is not yet ready; and therefore both may rejoice, the sleeping one, and the one awakened.

And this example has been followed by the poets of Persia and India—especially the Hindustani poets—and they have made their story in such form that it would be acceptable, not only to the seekers after truth, but also to those in all different stages of evolution.

Attar's best known work is *Mantiq at-Tayr* ("The Bird of
the Sky"), known in English as "The Conference of the
Birds," from which we have taken the idea of the "Blue
Bird"; and very few have understood the idea of the
"Blue Bird" or the "Bird of the Sky." It is a very ancient
teaching, through the use of the Persian word "sky."
This points out that every soul has a capacity which
may be called the sky, and this capacity can accommo-
date the world or the heaven, whatever it would par-
take of and hold in itself.

When one walks in the crowd, what does one see? One
sees numerous faces. I call them various attitudes. All
that you see in individuals, all that stands before you,
has expression, has atmosphere, has form. If you call it
by one name, it is the attitude: the attitude they have
towards life, right or wrong, good or bad. Whatever
attitude they have, they are themselves that attitude.
Does it not show how appropriate is the sky, which
means whatever you call it, whatever you may think it?

Plainly speaking, whatever one makes of oneself, one
becomes that—a source of happiness or unhappiness,
all is in man himself. When he is unaware of this, then
he is not able to arrange his life; and as he becomes
more acquainted with this secret, he gains a mastery,
and it is the process with which this mastery is attained
which is the only fulfillment of this life. It is that pro-
cess which is explained by Attar in his work with the
seven valleys through which this "Bird of the Sky" had
passed.

The first valley is that of the quest. How true it is that
every child is born with the tendency to search, to
know. What we call inquisitiveness or curiosity, it is
born in them, and it represents that inner feeling of

quest. This shows us that man is born with this, and he cannot be satisfied unless he has arrived at that satisfaction which means searching for that knowledge which he wishes to have.

No doubt, what prevents man from gaining that knowledge which his soul is really searching for is himself. It is his small self always standing against him, keeping him from the search of the only thing which is the seeking of every soul. And therefore it may be safe to say that there is no one in this world who is a worse enemy of man than himself.

In this search one thinks that one must perhaps find out from science, or from art, something which is behind it; and whether through material quest or spiritual, in the end one will arrive, and one must arrive, to that goal which is the goal of everyone. The scientists and engineers, people who are absorbed in making a search of material things and never think of spiritual things, even they, after making a great deal of search, they arrive very near to the same knowledge which is the ultimate knowledge; and therefore whatever a man may seem to us—materialist, atheist or agnostic—we cannot call him so, because in the end his goal is the same, his attainment is the same, if he really reaches the depth of knowledge, if he goes far enough. Whatever his search, he will come to the same goal.

And when one has searched enough and found something satisfactory, still he cannot enjoy that satisfaction unless there is one faculty open, and that is the faculty of love and devotion. Do we not see in our everyday life, that people of great intellect and wide interests very often seem to miss something? When it happens to be a couple where one is very intellectual, the other may feel there is something lacking to make their lives complete,

may feel that intellect alone is not enough. What is it?
It is the heart which balances life, and the absence of
which keeps life dry. It is just like the positive and
negative forces. Knowledge and heart: it is these two
things which make life balanced. If heart quality is very
strong and intellect lacking, then also life lacks balance.
Knowledge and heart quality must be developed in
balance.

And therefore, according to Attar, that faculty of
devotion, or quality of heart, is the Second Valley; and
the Third Valley is that knowledge which illuminates,
which comes by the help of the love element and the
intellect. It is that knowledge which is called spiritual
knowledge. Without the love quality developed, is man
incapable of having that knowledge? I will answer, yes.

There are fine lights and shades in one's life which
cannot be perceived and understood fully without
having touched the deeper side of life, which is the
devotional side. The person who has not in his life been
wholly grateful, he does not know its beauty. The one
who has not known gentleness, modesty, he cannot
appreciate its beauty or recognize it. No doubt, a
person of fine qualities is often ridiculed, if he happens
to be in a place where it is not understood, where it is a
foreign language. This shows there is a fineness in life
for which intellect alone is not sufficient. The heart
quality must become open.

A very intellectual man went to Jami and asked him to
take him as his pupil and give him initiation. Jami
looked at him and said, "Have you loved anybody?"
This man said, "No, I have not loved." Then Jami said,
"Go, and love first. Then come to me and I will show
you the way."

Love has its time in every stage of life. As a child, as a youth, as a grown-up person, in whatever stage of life one has reached, love is always asked for and love has always its part to perform. Whatever situation you are placed in, among friends or foes, among those who understand you and those who do not, in ease and in difficulty, in all places, at all times, it has its part to perform. And when one thinks, "I must not let the principle of love have its way, I must close myself against it," he imprisons his soul.

There is only one thing in the world, and that is pure unselfish love, which shows the sign of heaven, which shows the divine sign, which gives the proof of God. For all the noble qualities which are hidden in the soul will spring forth and come to bloom when love helps them and nurtures them. Man may have a great good in him, and he may be very intelligent, but as long as his heart is closed he cannot show that nobleness, that goodness, which is hidden in his heart.

And the psychology of the heart is such that once one begins to know the heart life is a continual phenomenon, every moment of life becomes a miracle. It throws a searchlight upon human nature, and all things become so clear to him that he does not ask for any greater phenomenon or miracle: it is a miracle in itself. What they call telepathy, thought-reading or clairvoyance—all these things come by themselves, where the heart is open.

If anyone is cold and stiff, he feels within himself as if he were in a grave. He is not living, he cannot enjoy this life for he cannot express himself. He cannot see the light and life outside; he is in his grave. And what keeps man back from development of heart quality? His exacting attitude. He wants to make a business of

love. He says, "If you will love me I will love you." As
soon as man exacts and measures and weighs his
favors, his services and all that he does for one whom
he loves, he does not know love.

Love sees the Beloved and nothing else. As Rumi says,
"Whether you love a human being or you love God,
there will come a day when all lovers, either of man or
of God, will be brought before the throne of Love and
the presence of that only Beloved will reign there."
What does this show? In loving our friend, in loving
our neighbor, even in the love that one shows to one's
enemy, one only loves God. And the one who says, "I
love God, but I cannot love man," he does not love God;
he cannot. It is like saying, "I love you very much, but I
do not like to look at your face."

And after this Third Valley, where the knowledge of
human nature, and of the fine feelings which are called
virtues, is attained, the next step is what is called in the
English language "annihilation." But what we call
destruction or annihilation is nothing but change.
Neither substance nor form nor spirit, nothing, is
absolutely destroyed—it is only changed.

But man does not like sometimes to change. He does
not know that he cannot live without change. He does
not like it, but he cannot live without it. There is not
one single moment of our life that change does not
come: whether we accept it or not, the change is there.
Destruction or annihilation or death might seem a very
different change, and yet there are a thousand deaths
that we die. Every disappointment, the moment when
our heart breaks—it is worse than death. Often our
experiences through life are worse than death, yet we
go through them. At the moment they seem unbear-
able; we think we cannot stand it, and yet we live.

If after dying a thousand deaths, we still live, there is nothing in the world to be afraid of. It is man's delusion, his own imagination: he makes it dreadful to himself. Can anyone kill life? If there is any death, it is for death; life will not die. To a Sufi someone went with a question; he said, "I have been puzzling for many, many years, and reading in books, and have not been able to find a definite answer—tell me, what happens after death?" The Sufi said, "Please ask that question of someone who is going to die. I am going to live."

The principle is that there is one sky, which is your own being. It is like the sky. In other words, you call it accommodation. And who has taken possession of this accommodation? A deluded ego which says, "I." It is deluded by this body and mind, and has called itself "individual." When a man has a ragged coat he says, "I am poor." In reality, his coat is poor—not he. What this capacity contains, that becomes his knowledge, his realization; and that limits him, forms that limitation which is the tragedy of every soul.

Now, this capacity either may be filled with self or may be filled with God. There is only place for one. Either we live with our limitation, or let God reign there in His unlimited being. In other words, we take away the home which always belonged to someone else and fill it with delusion and call it our own; and not only call it our own, but call it ourself. That is man's delusion, and all religious and philosophical teachings are given to rid man of this delusion, which deprives him of his spiritual wealth. Spiritual wealth is the greatest wealth, spiritual happiness the only happiness: there is no other happiness.

Once a person is able to disillusion himself, he arrives at the stage described in the Fourth Valley, the Valley of

Non-Attachment, and he is afraid. He thinks, "How can I give my home to someone else, even if it is God? This is my body, my mind, my home, my individuality. How can I give it away, even to God?"

But in reality, it is not something he can rely upon. It is delusion from top to toe, and subject to destruction. Does anything stand above destruction? Nothing. Then why fear to think for the moment that it is nothing. That natural fear of man comes because he is unaccustomed to face reality. He is so used to dreams, that he is afraid of reality. There is a fear in the minds of people of losing themselves, but they do not know that it is not losing one's self. It is losing illusion. And, really, they will find themselves when they lose this illusion. In this illusion, one has lost one's soul, and the process is to come out of it, to rise above it.

When the Fifth Valley, the Valley of Unity, is reached, by that time one has disillusioned one's self, and it is that act which is called in the Bible "rebirth," when the soul has become disillusioned. It is the birth of the soul. There is the birth of the body, and the birth of the soul. And how does this birth of the soul express itself? What does one feel? It first expresses itself in a kind of bewilderment with great joy. His interest in life is increased, all that he sees, he enjoys. He concerns himself little, but wonders at all things.

The bewilderment is such that it is a wonderful amusement to look at life. The whole world becomes to him a kind of stage, full of players. He then begins to amuse himself with the people of this world, as one might play with children and yet not be concerned with what they do, for he expects no better. If children do something different from the parents, they are not much concerned; they know it is the stage of the child's life and

43

one cannot expect any better of them. So with this man. Likes and dislikes, favor and disfavor, they interest him, but do not concern him.

And there is another stage. This bewilderment brings him to see the someone reflected who has taken possession of his heart: to see his Beloved in everyone, even in his enemy.

The Beloved is seen in all things. The bowl of poison given by the Beloved is not so bitter. Those who have sacrificed themselves and suffered for humanity, such as Christ, they have given to the world an example showing a soul that has reached the stage where even the enemy appears before the eyes of the God-conscious as friend, as his Beloved. And it is not an unattainable stage, because the soul is made of love, it is going towards the perfection of love. All the virtues man has learned, love has taught him. Therefore this world of good and bad, thorns and flowers, becomes nothing but a place of splendor.

The Sixth Valley, the Valley of Amazement, is the valley where he recognizes and understands what is behind things—the reason of all reasons, the cause of all causes. For all intuition and power develop in man with the unfoldment.

And the Seventh Valley, the Valley of Realization of God, is that peace which every soul is looking for, whether the spiritual or the material, seeking from morning until night for something which will give him peace. To some souls, that peace comes when asleep. But for the God-conscious, that peace becomes his home. No sooner has he closed his eyes, no sooner has he relaxed his body and stilled his mind, and lost from his consciousness the limited, than he begins to float in the unlimited spheres.

Translator's Introduction
Attar: Street-Sweeper

Rumi considered Attar and Sanai his poetic masters. He learned more from them than from his other predecessors. He said,

"Attar is the spirit and Sanai the eyesight.
We are the body that follows after."

Attar was very prolific. The number of his works is said to equal the number of suras in the *Qur'an*, ie., one hundred and fourteen. About thirty survive, among them, moral treatises, love stories, prose biographies of saints, a collection of quatrains, the magnificent *Conference of the Birds,* and the *Ilahinama* ("The Book of God").

Fariduddin Attar, as the name indicates, was a perfumist, and a doctor, as well as a poet. By his own account, he wrote *in his shop*, while seeing as many as five hundred patients a day! He examined them and prescribed as cures the herbal extractions which he himself prepared. His expertise was essences. He knew the medicinal efficacy of the balm of the fir and the attar of the rose, and he also knew the one substance at the core of all existence. He was a Sufi.

He was born in Nishapur in 1119, and he was killed there by the Mongol invaders in 1220. The dates here, though, are speculative, as is almost all the information in these introductions. A specific year of birth or death may be off by as much as ten or twenty years. Such are the discrepancies in the records. But Attar seems to have lived close to one hundred years. At the end of his life he met the boy Rumi, recognized the essence, embraced him and presented him with the *Asranama*, his book about the entanglement of the soul in the material world.

Most of the selections here are from the *Book of God*. It has a frame-story. A king asks his six sons what they wish for. The first wants a certain very beautiful girl for his wife. Another wants proficiency in the magical arts. Another wants Jamshid's cup, in which one can see what's going on every-

where in existence. The others desire the water of life,
Solomon's ring, and the secret elixir, all very sublime objects,
but the royal father tries with his stories and images to draw
each away from whatever he's attracted to, to an even higher
desire.

The shorts excerpts from *The Conference of the Birds* have
been adapted from C.S. Nott's translation.

The Woman Who Dressed as a Man

A traveler I met once knew a king
with six accomplished sons. They were masters
of many arts: philosophy, carpentry, languages,
planting, theology, and husbandry

They were conversant and adept in all,
but still full of pride, with no limits apparent.

The king seats them around him. "What do you want
from your lives? Do you have many wishes,
or one? Tell me, so I can see what you're learning."

The first son: "There is a girl as lively as thought,
and as graceful as the need to praise. If I
could be with her, I can't imagine wanting
anything else."

The father: "Understand. This is dangerous,
to live long within that urgent wish for her.
Be more like the woman who dressed as a man.
Separated from her husband, she became
a judge and a leader. Do you know
that story?

     Her face opens to the daylight,
while her hair, her back, the feel
of her skin, is night-essence immediate,
attar of dark. She is night and day
in one kind and faithful sign, a solid silver
apple put in a bowl of green apples.

Her husband leaves on a pilgrimage, a genuine hajj
to gain purity, patience, and a more constant
remembering of God. She adores his longing
for those qualities. The sky tilts
and dilates with their love.

He leaves her in the care of his younger brother,
a cautious, ungenerous man, who does his duty.

At first, he does his duty. Then he looks at her
differently. In a moment, he wants her.
A hundred lives of all his allotted lives
rush out in that changing. The spokes of a wheel
spinning in place without sound. He can't think.
He sits down beside her. *Please.* He's never
begged before. *Please.* "What of loyalty?
Yours to your brother, mine to my husband?"
Words mean nothing to him. "Death is not
more frightening than this forgetfulness,"
she says to him. But he must do something
with this wanting that he feels.

He brings in four strangers from the road,
vagrants. He pays them to lie believeably
that they've slept with this woman.
She's sentenced and taken to a high mountain pass.
There she's stoned from all sides
and left for dead. But she's not.

She begins to come to, little bits of her making moan.
Dawn. A Bedouin traveling alone sees her,
and says to the body, "Who are you, living
as though dead?" She can't speak. He puts her
across his donkey and carries her to his camp,
and tends her with tea and vegetable broth
on a pallet in his tent.

Beneath the bruising stones her face appears again.
And it happens with the Bedouin as with
the younger brother. He puts on his shirt each day
as if it were his shroud. "Become my wife,"
he begs. "Let me begin to live. I've never lived."

"Do not spoil your kindness to me
with this sudden need to make love.
Let me be a sister. I have a lover.
Other men to me are brothers."

A miracle happens, and slowly the Bedouin
agrees. He gives up this way of longing
and becomes a brother. As he does,
his black slave arrives back from a journey.
No one had expected him so soon.
The powerful servant sees the woman and wants her.
Words spring from his body, "I am night.
You are the moon. Why aren't we together?"

"Many ask me this. Why should you be different?"
The sudden love-need flames to hatred.
He rises in the middle of the night and goes
to the nursery where the Bedouin's child sleeps.
The Bedouin himself, you see, is married
and has one handsome infant child. The black man
severs the head of the Bedouin's child in the crib.
He leaves the two pieces of voiceless doll
for the mother to find, and he slips the unwiped
blade under the pillow of the woman he has wanted.

There's helpless screaming everywhere. The Bedouin
knows that the woman is innocent, but he knows too
that she can't stay there any longer
with the floating suspicions and grief.

He gives her three hundred dinars, and she starts out
walking toward the ocean. She comes to what
looks like a stage built by the road.
It's a gallows. A young man is standing on it
about to be hanged for not paying his taxes.
"How much does he owe?"

                              "Three hundred."

She gives it, and moves quickly away.
But he follows. One glimpse, and now
he wants her. A hand reaching through smoke.
"I can't turn away," he pleads. "Help me."

"This is what I get for my good deeds?
You must turn your head, or we cannot continue
on this road together. Look at the ocean
instead, the merchant ship at the dock.
Think of other things." His urgency
too turns to bitterness and lies.

"I have a slave girl," he tells the owner
of the ship. "There's no fault in her
except haughtiness. She's more conceited
than anyone I've ever seen. One hundred dinars."

He yells insults as they carry her on board.
Now the owner sees her face and wants her.
She kneels to the simple crew and begs them
for protection. She asks them to think of her
as they do their daughters, their mothers and sisters.
They do for a while, but soon the whole crew
is crazy to have her. They whisper at their work
like school children.

She feels the seawater turning to blood
around the ship. She prays the strongest prayer
of her life, to be free of the insane repetition
of men's lust. With her eyes closed,
flames rise from the boiling ocean.

When she wakes from praying, every man there
is a pile of fine ash wherever he stood.
She sweeps up the ashes and throws them
in the ocean. Then she sits down
to sew herself a man's clothing.

In a slight wind the ship drifts to another

harbor. The people on shore see a strange sight:
a slender young man seated alone on a ship
needing a crew of at least thirty and loaded
with tightly bound cargo. "How did you manage?"

"I will tell my story only to your king."
So she's led to a private audience, still disguised
as a young man. "A group of idle sailors
wanted me, the youngest man on the ship.

I prayed for their desire to be changed.
Fire rose off the water and consumed
all the men on board except me, and I
am not a man! I am a piece of charcoal
left over from the fire. And I understand
the warning which has been given to me.

I want none of the wealth on this ship.
Divide it however you wish. I ask only
one favor. Build me a small house
on the beach where I can worship alone.
The strict rule must be that no one,
no man or woman, clean or unclean,
can come near that house."

For years she lives there in solitude.
Then the king falls into a snare of disease.
He calls his ministers. "Let the young hermit
be the next ruler." A delegation goes
to the house on the beach. "But I have no wife,"
the hermit youth puts them off.

They bring hundreds of young girls with their mothers,
all blushing with bashfulness, waiting for his choice.

The hermit loosens her hair and reveals her breasts.
"Go back to your husbands and fathers,
Tell them I am a woman and that I have no desire
to govern." But still the ministers insist

that she be the ruler, and still she won't leave
her hut on the boundary between ocean and desert.

Instead, she becomes a healer. She asks
that paralytics come. When she breathes
on their hands and feet, they can move.

She asks for the blind. They begin to see,
when they hear her voice. When the king dies,
there is no government in this land,
just her healing presence.

Back at the starting point of this story,
her husband returns from Hajj to find his brother
strangely blind and unable to move his hands
or feet. Fixed to one spot, he can neither
see his food, nor reach out to take it.

But still he tells his lie about the wife's adultery.
The husband is in deep grief, but finally
from out of that, "On my journey I heard of a woman
who heals such as you are, blind, handless and footless."

He ties his brother over a donkey and sets out.
They meet the Bedouin. "My black slave," he says
"is in the same condition." Two donkeys with human
baggage and good men beside, they meet the tax-evader,
who is also now blind and paralyzed.

It's a three donkey caravan that she sees coming.
She veils herself. "Can you heal these men?"

"Yes, but only if they confess what deep offence
has caused their condition. Otherwise they must
stay as they are."
                    "I'd rather remain blind
and helpless," says the younger brother. For hours
they try to convince him to say aloud his sin.
Finally he tells it. Nothing is held back: his lust,
his lying, his brother's wife beneath the stones.

"Crippled and blind with what I've done, kill
or forgive me. I'm at your mercy."

Then the Bedouin's slave says, "I too am afraid to
speak."

The Bedouin: "I forgive you already, whatever it is."

"I beheaded your child in the crib."

Then the tax-evader blurts out, "A woman redeemed me
from hanging, and I sold her into slavery."

The healing woman prays for them, and they are healed.
She sends all away except her husband.
She removes the veil. He faints. He revives.
"I once had a wife, and you resemble her exactly
in each detail of your face, my love
now dissolved in the ground."

"I don't *resemble* her. I am your wife,
not dead, and not unfaithful. God brought me
to this place, and now you."

They fall prostrate in worship
on the sand, one mind in both.

The husband calls an assembly of the people
and tells the entire story.

The slave, the younger brother, and the tax-evader
listen, filled with shame and with a new rejoicing.

Then the wife appoints her husband as king
and makes the Bedouin prime minister.

She gives gifts of great value
to the younger brother, the tax-evader
and the slave, so the men have their new wealth
and a government to administer.

She herself returns to the hut
beside the ocean to continue as before

her constant remembering of God.

Listening to the Reed Flute

There's a blind man on the road saying,
Allah, Allah. Sheikh Nuri runs to him,
"What do you know of Allah? And if you know,
why do you stay alive?" The sheikh keeps on,
beside himself with ecstatic questions.
Then he runs into a low place, where
a reedbed has recently been cut down.

He falls and gets up, falls again,
floundering on the sharp reed-ends.
People come and find him dead, the ground
wet with blood and written on every reed-tip,
the word *Allah.* This is the way one must
listen to the reed flute. Be killed
in it and lie down in the blood.

Street-Sweeper

"Street-sweeper, something about you
bothers me. You walk the streets
looking for what you haven't lost.
You can never find that!"

The street-sweeper answers, "And even stranger,
if I do not find what I have not lost,
I get frantic with worry."

One does not find or lose,
keep silent or speak. Neither
this nor that, but both.

Looking for Your Own Face

Your face is neither infinite nor ephemeral.
You can never see your own face,
only a reflection, not the face itself.

So you sigh in front of mirrors
and cloud the surface.

It's better to keep your breath cold.
Hold it, like a diver does in the ocean.
One slight movement, the mirror-image goes.

Don't be dead or asleep or awake.
Don't be anything.

What you most want,
what you travel around wishing to find,
lose yourself as lovers lose themselves,
and you'll *be* that.

The Newborn

Muhammed spoke to his friends
about a newborn baby, "This child
may cry out in its helplessness,
but it doesn't want to go back
to the darkness of the womb.

And so it is with your soul
when it finally leaves the nest
and flies out into the sky
over the wide plain of a new life.
Your soul would not trade that freedom
for the warmth of where it was.

Let loving lead your soul.
Make it a place to retire to,
a kind of monastery cave, a retreat
for the deepest core of being.

Then build a road
from there to God.

Let every action be in harmony with your soul
and its soul-place, but don't parade
those doings down the street
on the end of a stick!

Keep quiet and secret with soul-work.
Don't worry so much about your body.
God sewed that robe. Leave it as is.

Be more deeply courageous.
Change your soul."

Mysticism

The sun can only be seen by the light
of the sun. The more a man or woman knows,
the greater the bewilderment, the closer
to the sun the more dazzled, until a point
is reached where one no longer is.

A mystic knows without knowledge, without
intuition or information, without contemplation
or description or revelation. Mystics
are not themselves. They do not exist
in selves. They move as they are moved,
talk as words come, see with sight
that enters their eyes. I met a woman
once and asked her where love had led her.
"Fool, there's no destination to arrive at.
Loved one and lover and love are infinite."

From *The Conference of the Birds*

The hoopoe, the crested one who acts as guide, tells about
the fifth valley on the Way, the Valley of Unity:

"There everything is broken to pieces and reformed.
All lift their heads in that place
from one collar.

And since the Being I speak of is beyond
unity and numbering, beyond
before and after, and since all that is visible
vanishes to nothing, nothing
can be spoken or contemplated.

In this valley the spiritual traveler disappears,
and the unique Being will manifest.

The part becomes the whole,
and in the school of the secret,
what is knowledge?

Intellect hesitates on that threshold
like a blind child.

And after the Valley of Unity comes the Valley
of Bewilderment, and sadness, and a burning
eagerness. Day and night at once,
fire, and yet depression.

And if the traveler here is asked,
'Do you exist? Where are you? Are you immortal?'
He will say with absolute certainty,
'I know nothing. I do not know
who I am. I am in love,
but I do not know with whom.
My heart is empty and full at the same time!'"

At the end of their pilgrimage the thirty birds (*si-murgh* in Persian) come to a door.

The chamberlain, having tested their clarity
with questions and their intensity
with refusals, opened the door
and drew aside the hundreds of veils,
and a new reality was revealed.

And a writing was given to them.
They read it, and as they read,
they understood their state.

They grew peaceful and detached,
and aware that the great Simurgh
was there among them and that the new life
they had wanted was beginning inside that presence.

Everything they had done before was washed away,
and in each other's faces they saw
the inner world. They did not know
if they were still themselves,
or if they had become God.

At last, in a deep state of contemplation,
they knew they were the Simurgh,
and that the Simurgh was the thirty birds.

They saw both as one and the same being.
No experience can equal that experience.

They gave themselves up to meditation,
and after a little they asked the Simurgh,
without using language, to reveal the mystery
of the unity and the multiplicity of beings.

Without speaking, the answer came, "This majesty
is a mirror. If you approach as thirty birds,
that's what you will find. Forty or fifty
birds would come and see forty and fifty.

And although you are now completely changed,
you see yourselves as you were before.

You did well to be astounded and impatient
and doubting and full of wonder.

Lose yourselves in me joyfully,
and you will find yourselves."

And they did, as a shadow disappears
in sunlight, and that is all.

RUMI:
Birdsong Moving Through Us Like Rain

JELALUDDIN RUMI

B eloved ones of God,

My subject today is Jelaluddin Rumi, the greatest poet
the world has ever known: a poet whose message, in
his life and work both, marks a distinct line as a new
era, a new step in Sufism, which was the most ancient
school of Mystics and Philosophers, and which
originated from the ancient mystic school of Egypt.
The first and best known initiate of that particular
school was Abraham, the father of the three great reli-
gions of the world: Judaism, the Christian religion and
the Islamic religion.

Jelaluddin Rumi gave a new life and a new form to the
mystical current, and it is from his time that the Sufi
mystic culture spread throughout the world. The
reason was that he was not only a mystic and dreamer,
but he was the most learned man of his time—a great
statesman and politician, at the head of the law of his
country (like a chief judge). And he had a great reputa-
tion among the people as a most learned man: a man of

reason, most practical and wide awake; a master of
theology. In point of fact, he was the man of the day in
his country. He had read poetry, and some of the
poems of Attar, but his learning was based upon
theological training.

The story of his life is most wonderful, especially his
awakening to the Sufi ideal. Once he was sitting at
leisure with his manuscripts. At that time there was no
printing, no books, so manuscripts were treasures. And
there entered a man in rags. From the appearance of
that man anyone would have thought that he was a
beggar, a pauper; at the same time he walked like a
king. And instead of a salutation of any sort, the first
thing he did was to remove all the manuscripts that
were there.

Rumi could not understand a man in rags coming into
the house of a leading citizen and throwing away all the
manuscripts he had so valued. But he was a great man;
he did not allow himself to express his annoyance with
this conduct. He was perfectly self-disciplined; only he
asked him, "What do you wish to do?" And this man
said, "What are you reading? Is it not finished yet? You
have been reading all your life and still it is not finished.
You are reading in small pages which cannot contain
what the book of life is continually revealing, and this
has absorbed all your life. What little is left, is that also
to be absorbed in this?"

Rumi said, "What is there to think about? What do you
wish to point out?"

"I wish to ask you if you have considered what is the
purpose of your life. Is this position you occupy just
now, this rank and position and fame, is this the pur-
pose? What are you growing to, what are you looking
forward to? What aim and object do you have before

you? Is your life so momentary as one sees it from birth
to death, which is not more than four days, or is it a
continual life? If it is continued, where is it continued?
If this exalted position belongs to you now, it once be-
longed to somebody else, and it will again belong to
somebody else. Even if it is something important, it re-
ally does not belong to you. And these helpless manu-
scripts, they are subject to destruction one day. If that is
your wisdom, how long will it last?

"Have you looked into the manuscript of your heart?
Have you looked into life, to see what life is continually
teaching everyone? You have worshipped God—have
you talked with Him? Have you seen Him? Have you
really known Him? What is the use of your worship? A
religion that all your life you have followed, do you
know where it came from? What is the source of it? Do
you wish to live as everybody in this world is living, not
knowing for what they are living? The horses and cam-
els also live and they are busy, but there is no credit in
their being busy. The credit of one's occupation is in
the virtue of the occupation. Have you thought of the
virtue of your occupation, is it reliable? If it is a passing
virtue, it is not a reliable virtue."

This made Rumi think, and this moved Rumi to tears.
And the personality of that ragged man, what it poured
out to Rumi! It was like unlimited wealth. Rumi had
nothing to say. He was overwhelmed with all that this
chance stranger had told him, and as certainly as this
chance stranger had come, so certainly he had gone.
When he had gone, Rumi said, "That God Whom I have
worshipped all my life, today I saw him in human form."

The man in rags was Shams-i-Tabriz, and Rumi was so
impressed by what he had said to him, that he followed
him. The first thing Rumi had to meet with was bitter

criticism on all sides. No one could understand how a man so learned, a man of such ability and education, could spend his time always walking with this ragged stranger. But wherever he walked or stood, there Rumi walked and stood; and if a hundred people stood around, or a thousand people stood around, he did not care.

This seeming misfortune ended in the resignation of Rumi from his position. He could no longer hold his position with the increasing criticism, and he had no time to explain to everyone. He was too much absorbed in listening to Shams-i-Tabriz. He had no time to argue. All his time was taken to understand what Shams-i-Tabriz said. And this apparent misfortune ended in a sudden shock: one day, in the same way as he had come, so suddenly Shams-i-Tabriz disappeared.

Then Rumi found himself alone, and yet not alone. In the world of thought that was surrounding him, Rumi could see nothing but the deep ideas that Shams-i-Tabriz had given him. He had opened his outlook on life. It was more than what he said, it was something awakened and opened in the heart of Rumi. It was a kind of expansion of Rumi's consciousness. It was not a learning or a teaching, more than that—it was a phenomenon.

Yet Rumi, like a child, had absorbed every word that fell from the lips of Shams-i-Tabriz and treasured them in his heart. He could not dry his tears for days and days, and for weeks and weeks. He thought if it was good-ness, it was not goodness as we conceive of it: it was the greatest goodness that could exist. It was a divine mercy and compassion. If it was education, it was not as man knows education: it was a shower of knowl-edge. It was like a key to heaven and earth. It was something which words could not explain.

Now, on the one side Rumi had lost his position, and to some extent his reputation, in the eyes of the world and even in the eyes of those near and dear to him, because they could not understand. And on the other hand the only one he had to lean upon was Shams-i-Tabriz, and he was gone too.

Therefore, naturally the life of Rumi became a life of contemplation, a life of studying nature, and a life of devotion to a divine personality that had once appeared before him. So all that is necessary for the spiritual life came into the life of Rumi, all that was needed to tread the spiritual path. Therefore, the life of Rumi became the kind of life that Sufis for many centuries have followed.

At times when his thoughts and feelings made him think there was a kind of congestion on his heart he would ask the musicians to come and sing, in the meditative way of singing. They sang mostly the words of Shams-i-Tabriz and Rumi: words of the heart of man waking to higher devotion, words pointing out the divine ways of life and the secret of concentration.

That custom exists even now in India and Persia: there are times when the beautiful words of such great poets as Rumi and Shams-i-Tabriz are sung with music, and the people sit there and listen and enjoy and are benefited by it, and they are tuned to that pitch where they can get the real benefit out of that music—and this assembly is considered the most sacred assembly, when the sacred music is played.

From this a new way was found which was different from the existing Yogism in the East. Where this way was different was in that tendency to look at the whole

life as an illusion—which is true—and to try to get de-
tached from it, that one may not be caught by this life
which keeps man back: this tendency made a sort of
wall between the Yogi and the world. Rumi's way of
contemplation was after the contemplation of his
teacher and what he said, and the truth that was given
to him: after looking at life in that way, then to melt it
all with the vibrations of music.

It is all attachment and yet above attachment, which
means on the sea and yet not in the sea. It is the same
symbology as that is used in the Bible, the walking of
Christ on the water. There are three ways of living life:
walking upon the water, swimming in the water, and
the third way is to be drowned. Those who are
drowned are those attached to the material world, and
this attachment in the end sinks them. Then there is a
way of going through life which is like swimming. And
the third way is walking on the water; that is, going
through all things and yet not touching them, standing
above them; to be in the world but not of it.

And this has won the greatest reward for the Sufis of
the East, and that reward was the charm of their person-
alities. The feeling developed by divine contemplation
enabled them to spread the waves of love and affection,
and to look at life with optimism and hope, and with
hope to make the best of it; and if it is hard and disap-
pointing, still to make the best of it. To bend all material
towards its best purpose and to make every aspect of life
turn into the means of the fulfilment of the whole cre-
ation, that no material be lost.

To the Sufi, saint and sinner both come close to him.
Friend or enemy, he is the well-wisher and lover of
both—for behind the friend and the enemy he sees his
Beloved. His power over his enemy is great, because his

enemy cannot longer hold him so when he sees in him a friend. It is the contemplation of the Beloved that the Sufi carries ever with him. It is the one Being he knows, and he is always in His presence. He cannot keep enmity; the fire of his love burns up the sting of enmity.

The greatest pity of the day is how little we understand the word "love." Very often man understands by love no more than a bargain: if you give me sixpence, I will give you a shilling. That is not love; it is too small when one expects a return. The first lesson man should learn from love: there is no "I." "I" is the very enemy of love. People think there cannot be a greater loss than losing "I"—if they only knew, there cannot be a greater gain. Because when the "I" is lost, then all is gained.

The whole process of esoteric or spiritual attainment is this: to give up "I" and gain all. This is the only secret which is at the back of all religions, philosophies and mysticism, if one can understand it. Little can be said about it; it is to practise. In every little thing one does, this small "I" comes up, and to keep it subdued takes time and practice. The Sufi teachings have all been given for this. How can this little "I" be kept down, that it may not spring up and stand in the way of one's growth? Friends, we may have many enemies and many who oppose us. But if we looked at life closely and understood it, we should find that we have no greater enemy than ourselves. All that we wish is pushed away by this "I."

And Rumi has made a most beautiful picture of this philosophy. He begins his most wonderful work, *The Mathnawi*, by saying: "Listen to the flute and hear what it says. What is it that comes from the flute that wins your soul, that pierces through your heart?" Then he gives us an example: the flute, a piece of reed that was cut from its stem and was brought away from its origin, has its story to tell. It is hollow, its heart is empty; but besides that emptiness, several holes were made to its heart, that it may give all the notes that it is asked to give out, from the lowest to the highest note. And then he goes on to say, "But what is this flute and where is its voice?" The one is under the lips of the Beloved, and the other is singing to the world outside.

There he leaves it for man to solve the riddle. There he has given a picture of man. Man is a piece of bamboo cut away from its stem: that stem is whole, is perfect; the piece is imperfect. Life has cut holes to its heart that it may sound all the notes: once the holes are made, it begins to give the music that wins the souls of men.

Besides this example of the flute, there is one verse of Rumi's which is most beautiful: "Many became my friends through love who have not understood what it is in me that brings me closer. If they only knew this, they would solve the whole problem of life." What does he mean by this? He means that it is the hollowness and emptiness of the reed that brings it nearer to the lips of the divine love. And so it is with the heart of man: the heart of man is the flute of God, and it touches the lips of God when it is empty. As long as it is not empty, it does not touch the lips of God.

All revelation, the whole secret, can be found in the heart of man. There is nowhere else man can find the secret of life except within himself. No doubt Rumi has shown in one of his verses the way to the goal, in which he says, "If you wish to attain God, and at the same time to attain to all things of this world, you should not strive for it, for it is not possible."

This does not mean that all things in this world must be renounced. But if the position in life presents a condition where there are two things to do, either to renounce the very object that we have within us, or to renounce something on the outside—it is better to renounce that something on the outside, and keep that object within. This is the study of everybody in this world. Everyone has good intentions; everyone wishes to get the best there is in life. But the first place where man finds difficulty is in something that he values the most, and yet he does not know if it exists. And there is something else that he values less, but at the same time he knows it is.

And the value of all religion, philosophy and mysticism is to help man to perceive that object within. It is something your ideal only can touch; something only known to your consciousness—and even your consciousness cannot make it intelligible enough for your mind to grasp. And to hold to this in the midst of so many things which are intelligible, this is the test.

Man thinks, "Shall I take this that I know, or shall I go in pursuit of something of whose existence I am not certain? Shall I not be at a loss?" For modern life teaches commercialism. Man hesitates to do something in which there is no gain. It does not appeal to him. Virtue is not precious to him. But in reality it is the greatest gain, because nothing else in the world can satisfy.

Therefore, in the end one comes to the conviction that there is only one thing in the world worthwhile, and that is spiritual attainment, or the attainment of God. Only what one needs is to strengthen the faculty of faith, which stands by its own strength even when you touch an ideal which has nothing else to hold it.

Friends, the difference between the world and God can be seen by understanding the difference between the sun and the things of the earth. All things of the earth must have something to hold them—if not they fall down. But the sun, nothing is holding it; it stands itself, supported by nothing. And so with God. All things of the world are supported by reasoning. If there is anything that stands without reasoning, it is God. And why is it so? Becaue His true being is your self.

It is only seeing your self in its perfection which is the vision of God. But at the same time, it must be understood that there are two ways of looking at it. God, the inner and true God, we cannot even call "God." It would be an error if we tried to give Him a name, it would be limited. If we call Him "One," it is addition and division, which God has not. Words cannot explain. If one is to explain the real God, his explanation is "silence."

There is another way of looking at it. In order to attain to that God, we must make a God within ourselves. Therefore, the God of each one is different. By giving God a personality and by thinking of that personality, we lose our own personality. By raising Him to a height, we are raised to a height. Until it so happens that the man-made God carries one along until he touches the real God. The man-made God protects, and the real God lives.

This is the fulfilment of all religion, all philosophy, all mysticism. And it is this realization of truth which closes the lips of those who have realized it. This is the great secret of life.

73

Translator's Introduction
Rumi: Birdsong Moving Through Us Like Rain

Unlike other figures in this collection Rumi's life is well documented. A hundred and forty-seven personal letters have survived! I won't try to re-tell the external sequence of his famous life-story here. He came of a spiritually illustrious line. His father Bahauddin was also a powerfully original mystic. In the *Maarif*, a kind of visionary diary, the father describes how God would kiss and absorb him like a lover in the night. Rumi's own realization of nearness is the most authentic region of his life. Outer events to a mystic are not nearly so salient as the inner changing. Not the poetry, nor the turn, no action is so important as Rumi's openhearted emptiness. There was the long conversation with Shams (sohbet is the Turkish word, *toucher l'essence* in French; they were together at the core of being); then the separation, and the continued "talking" in the poetry. Rumi endured a presence beyond the personal. Some go silent at that point. Others can only breathe *Allah, Allah*. Rumi, though, was still in command of a full cultural orchestra, all instruments intact.

Several poems here mention the reed flute. Rumi has what amounts to a theory of language associated with this instrument. The reed flute says one thing through its empty cane center: *I want to go back to the canebrake*. No matter how intricate it gets, Rumi says, language underneath all its sounds is the one hollow resonance of separation, the wail of the human condition at being uprooted from the whole. This is a truth and a puzzlement to Rumi. Why isn't there a double note, he wonders, along with the complaint, a strand of praise for the skill of the craftsman who not only plucked the reed from the reedbed, but also fashioned the bare cylinder into a ney, the human form with its nine holes.

The poems here include examples of most of the forms that Rumi worked in. Some quatrains (the short poems), two ghazals (the intermediate length odes), a wedding piece, one prose segment from the *Discourses*, and several longer pieces from the *Mathnawi*, the incomparable fifty-two thousand line work which Rumi dictated to Husam, his scribe, for the last twelve years of his life.

The story from the *Discourses* is one that Shams of Tabriz told. Shams was Rumi's teacher and his door into presence. They met on a street in Konya. Shams asked, "Who is greater, Bestami or Muhammed, for Bestami said, 'How great is my glory!' and Muhammed said, 'We do not praise You as You should be praised.'" Rumi felt the depth the question came from and fell off the donkey he was riding. Reviving, he answered, "Muhammed is greater, because Bestami took one gulp and his thirst was quenched. Whereas for Muhammed the Way was continually unfolding." Shams realized that he had found the companionship he'd been searching for his entire life. The mystery of their Friendship is the source and the subject of the poetry.

We Point to the New Moon

This time when you and I sit here, two figures
with one soul, we're a garden,
with plants and birdsong moving through us
like rain.
>   The stars come out. We're out
of ourselves, but collected. We point
to the new moon, its discipline and slender joy.

We don't listen to stories
full of frustrated anger. We feed
on laughter and a tenderness
we hear around us,
>   when we're together.

And even more incredible, sitting here in Konya,
we're this moment in Khorasan and Iraq.

We have these forms in time,
and another in the elsewhere
that's made of this closeness.

The Reed Flute

Listen to the story told by the reed,
of being separate.

"Since I was cut from the reedbed,
I have made this crying sound.

Anyone separated from someone he loves
understands what I say.

Anyone pulled from a source
longs to go back.

At any gathering I am there, mingling
in the laughing and the grieving,

a friend to each, but few
will hear the secrets hidden

within the notes. No ears for that.
Body flowing out of spirit,

spirit up from body. We can't conceal
that mixing, but it's not given us

to see the soul." The reed flute
is fire, not wind. Be nothing.

Hear the love-fire tangled
in the reed notes, as bewilderment

melts into wine. The reed is a friend
to all who want the fabric

torn and drawn away. The reed is
hurt and salve combining.

Intimacy and longing for
intimacy in one song.

A disasterous surrender,
and a fine love, together.

The one who secretly hears this
is senseless.

A tongue has one customer,
the ear.

The power of a cane flute comes
from its making sugar in the reedbed.

Whatever sound it has
is for everyone.

Days full of wanting, let them go by
without worrying that they do.

Stay where you are, inside
such a pure, hollow note.

Full Moon, Bilal

There is a small meal before daybreak
during Ramadan. It's called the *sahur*,
and traditionally, a drum-call announces it.

It's midnight. A man sits beside the gate
of an empty building, drumming steadily
the *sahur* drumbeat.

Someone comes by. "Wait a minute!
In the first place, the *sahur* happens at dawn,
or just before. Midnight is no time
for this noise. And secondly,
there's no one around! Why beat a drum
if no one will hear? Is there some
hidden intelligence in what you do?

The midnight *sahur* drummer answers,
"Are you through with your questions?
For you, it may be the middle of the night.
For me, dawn is very near. To my eyes,
every night looks like daytime.

To you, this gate feels like iron,
but to the hands of a great artisan
it feels workable like wax.

To you, a mountain is solid matter piled up.
To David, a mountain is a master-musician
he can learn from. To you, a column
is inanimate stone. To Muhammed,
it is a friend about to surrender to God,
that alive! To some, the particles
of this world seem dead, but they're not.
They have knowledge. They make decisions!

And you ask, 'Why beat this drum where nobody is?'
When pilgrims go to Mecca, they sell their houses
and give alms, and they never ask when they arrive
at the Kaaba, 'Is anybody home?'

Whoever is filled with the Friend's light
knows what fills any emptiness.

Wherever such a one is,
the Kaaba rises to be.

A True Human Being is always standing
there. Others only visit.

Pilgrims cry out, 'Lord!'
and there's never an answering cry,
yet they don't complain. Why is this?

They know that that which causes them
to say 'Lord!' is itself the 'Here I am'
blessing that they came for.

Inside any deep asking is the answering.
Like that, something lets me know
that I should be drumming
the *sahur* here.

Some people go to war.
Some endure painful difficulties.
Some wait patiently.

Everybody does service of some sort.
Mine is drumming at this gate
where the only listener is God,

the One who buys a dirty sack
and gives inner light in return,
who takes the dissolving ice of this body
and gives a vast countryside,
the One who receives our grief
and changes it to a lovely river.

For one sigh, the most illustrious prize.

Sell your old rags in this market.
Get a silver city in exchange.

When you have doubts about this kind of trading,
read the experts, the prophets.
They've been doing this so long
that a warehouse as big as a mountain
would not contain the goods."

Bilal is being whipped by his employer!
Whipped with thorn branches in the heat of summer.
Blood shows with each blow. "Why must you
take time off to worship when you work
for me!" All Bilal can say
in his ecstatic state is,
    ONE!
                With each downstroke of thorns,
ONE!
Abu Bakr, passing by, catches the scent
of a lover of God, and afterwards, privately,
he tells Bilal, "Keep your longing secret.
This love is between you and God."

"Please pardon my display," says Bilal.
The next day, on some business or other,
Abu Bakr is in the same section of town,
and he hears the same sounds, the scourge
of thorns and the response,
            ONE!

                The warmth
of that great love comes again immediately
into Abu Bakr's chest, but again
he takes Bilal aside and warns him
to keep his ecstasy silent.

Bilal again repents, and every time
he feels inclined to cry out, he repents,
until finally he snaps, and gives up repenting
altogether, thinking, "I am so filled with love
that I have no room for repentence!

I'm straw in a strong wind.
How could I possibly know where I'll end up?
New moon, full moon, half moon,
I'm just following the sun. The moon
doesn't care about being fat or thin!

All it cares about is the sun!
Resurrection is happening now!

Should I worry about whether
I'm strong willed enough to obey
some rule of behavior?

In the hand of love I'm like a cat in a bag,
lifted up and whirled around overhead.

That's how much control I have over circumstances.
Whitewater carries me along. I am a millstone
turning day and night, moaning and creaking.

By my turning, you know the power and motion
of the invisible river. The beloved friend
is a river. The nightsky is a waterwheel
revolving in that. The love-river
doesn't rest. In it, if you grab a branch,
the river breaks it. Any attachment you have,
take hold strongly and let it be snapped off!

If you can't see the huge sky-turnings,
look at the broken sticks moving by,
and the foam-bubbles around you.

The giddy wind, the constantly reaching up
of the ocean, these are parts of the same motion.

The sun and the moon are two oxen
going patiently around
this grinding millstone earth.

The stars run more eccentrically
from house to house telling our news,
whether good or bad or in between.

Sometimes it's freezing, sometimes honey-warm.
Sometimes we're separate, sometimes together.

Everything keeps changing. How could we not?
We're like a horse that somebody important owns,
now confined in a stall, now out on a road,
now tied to a post, now set loose running
in a pasture, now prancing before a crowd.

But, remember, there *are* dangerous moments,
like those two points on the moon's path
called the Dragon's Tail, where an eclipse
occurs. Don't get cut off from sunlight!

Lightning snaps out like a whip,
'Not that way! This! Listen to me!'

Don't toy with things that block your light.
As you give those up... but enough of this
good-and-bad talk. Whether *open* or *secret*,
it's New Year's Day! Water rushes back
into the riverbed. A king walks our street.
A drum says, 'Don't worry about repentence.'

The nightwatchman falls asleep.
We pawn everything we own.

Red within red within red.
I hear the singing coming this way,
A thornwhipping becomes a bouquet of roses."

Bilal is a sieve.
Soul-scent drifts through him.

Muhammed arrives. "Bilal you are so dear
to me, so dear."

Abu Bakr hears the inner speech of Bilal
and says, "You're right. You need never
repent again. Now. Repent
of your repenting!"

Say Who I Am

I am dust particles in sunlight.
I am the round sun.

To the bits of dust I say, *Stay*,
To the sun, *Keep moving*.

I am morning mist,
and the breathing of evening.

I am wind in the top of a grove,
and surf on the cliff.

Mast, rudder, helmsman, and keel,
I am also the coral reef they founder on.

I am a tree with a trained parrot in its branches.
Silence, thought, and voice.

The musical air coming through a flute,
a spark off a stone, a flickering

in metal. Both candle,
and the moth crazy around it.

Rose, and the nightingale
lost in the fragrance.

I am all orders of being, the circling galaxy,
the evolutionary intelligence, the lift,

and the falling away. What is,
and what isn't. You who know

Jelaluddin, You the One
in all, say who

I am. Say I
am You.

Blessing the Marriage Of the daughter of
Saladin Zarkub to Nizam al-din Kattat.

This marriage be wine with halvah, honey dissolving in milk.

This marriage be the leaves and fruit of a date tree.

This marriage be women laughing together for days on end.

This marriage, a sign for us to study.

This marriage, beauty.

This marriage, a moon in a light-blue sky.

This marriage, this silence fully mixed with spirit.

A Story Shams Told

Our Master Shams used to tell the story of a great caravan going toward a certain place, where they found no habitation and no water. There was a deep hole, but no bucket and no rope. To test for fresh water, they tied a kettle to a rope of their own and let it down. It struck something, and they pulled, but the kettle broke away. They sent down another and lost it as well. After that they lowered thirsty volunteers from the caravan, but they disappeared too!

There was a wise man there. He said, "I will go down." He was nearly to the bottom when a terrible black creature appeared. "I can never escape from you," said the man to the monster, "but I hope at least to stay aware, so I can see what's happening to me."

"Don't tell me long stories," said the black creature. "You're my prisoner. You'll never leave, unless you answer one question."

"Ask it."

"Where is the best place?"

The wise man reflected, "I am totally helpless here. If I say Baghdad or some other beautiful place, it may be that I will insult his hometown by not mentioning it." So he replied, "The best place for a man to live is where he feels at home. If that's a hole in the middle of the earth, then that's it."

"Well said. You're a rare human being. Because of your blessing, I'll set the others free in your care and give you authority over the world. I'll take no more prisoners, and I'll release the waters of this well."

Shams told this story for its inner meaning, which might be phrased in other ways, but those attached to traditional forms will accept this version. They're so hard to talk to. Tell just a slightly different parable, and they won't listen at all.

Dying

The prophet Muhammed was and is
many spiritual resurrections at once.
Here and *now*, spendable cash!

He dissolved out of time, and twice-born,
became a living resurrectioning.

But people would come and ask, "*How long
does it take to be born again?*"

He would answer without speaking,
with the eloquence of his inner state,
Die before you die.

Until you become a rebirth,
you won't know what that is.

It's the same with anything.
You don't understand until you *are*
what you're trying to understand.

Become reason, and you'll know it perfectly.
Become love and be a burning wick
at the center of yourself.

I would make this very plain,
if someone were ready for what I have to tell.
Figs are cheap around here! Mystical knowledge
is easy to come by. All you need
is just to arrive, as a bird
who loves figs lights
in a fig tree.

Everybody in the world is dying.
Everybody is in a death agony.

Listen to what anyone says
as though it were the last words
of a father to his son.

Listen with that much compassion,
and you'll never feel jealousy
or anger again.

They say, "Everything that's coming will come."
Understand, it's here right now!

The friend you're talking to is speaking
through his death-rattle, this moment.

If you're too self-absorbed for this kind of listening,
remember there is a Great Incapacitator.

God gave you this inability for some reason.
Ask why. Say, "I have tried,
but I'm in a losing business.

I did what you warned me not to.
I claimed not to love the world's images,
but I've been worshipping them.

Should I think more about death
than about God?"

In autumn, the source of the dead leaves
is the buried, live root.

O Origin of Dead Leaves, for years
you've beat the drum to tell me.

Only now that I'm dying
do I realize that I'm going to die!

Death's throat is raw and exhausted
with shouting at me. The dead-drum
is split and broken from being struck
with such astounding force.

I've been so woven into the mesh
of my trivial errands, that only now
do I begin to hear the mystery
of dying everywhere.

New Moon, Hilal

You've heard about the qualities of Bilal.
Now hear about the thinness of Hilal,
which is more advanced than Bilal.

He denied his *nafs* more than some of you
who move backward, from being an illumined globe
toward becoming again an opaque stone.

Remember the story of the young guest
who came before a certain king. "And how old are you,
my lad? Tell the truth now. Say it out."

"Eighteen, well seventeen.   Sixteen.
Actually uh, fifteen."

"Keep going! You'll end up
in your mother's womb."

Or the man who went to borrow a horse.
"Take the grey."
                "No, not that one."
"Why?"
          "It goes in reverse. It backs up."
"Then turn its tail toward your home."

The beast you ride is your various appetites.
Change your wantings. When you prune
weak branches, the remaining fruit
get tastier. Lust can be re-directed,
so that even when it takes you backward,
it goes toward shelter.

A strong intention can make "two oceans wide"
be the size of a blanket, or "seven hundred years"
the time it takes to walk to someone you love.

True seekers keep riding straight through,
whereas big, lazy, self-worshipping geese
unload their pack animals in a farmyard
and say, "This is far enough."

Do you know the story of the travelers
who came to a village in early spring?
There's an abandoned house with an open door.

"Why don't we wait for this cold spell to pass,
this *old woman's chill*, they call it.
Let's put our baggage in here and rest."

A deep voice from inside, "No. Unload outside,
then enter. This is a meeting hall
of great dignity!"

There are such secret sanctuaries.

Although he worked in a stable as a groom,
Hilal was an enlightened master.

His employer did not understand Hilal's state.
He knew up and down and north-south-east-west,
the evidence of the senses, but nothing else.

The color of the ground is in front of us,
but prophetic light is hidden.

One person sees a minaret, but not the bird
perched there. A second person sees the bird,
but not the hair it carries. A third
sees minaret, bird, and hair.

Until you can see the thread of the hair,
the knot of awareness will not be loosened.

The body is the minaret. Obedience,
the bird. Or three hundred birds, or two,
however you want it. The second person
sees the bird, and only the bird.

The hair is the secret
that belongs to the bird.

No nest built with such material
will go unused A song-thread flows
continuously out of the bird.

Try to see this bird on its clay tower,
and also the hair floating in its beak.

Hilal becomes ill. Nine days he lies sick
in the stable. No one notices,
except the prophet Muhammed, peace
and blessing be upon him.
He comes to visit.

Hilal's employer is ecstatic.
With elaborate ceremony he emerges
from his upstairs room and kisses the ground
in front of the prophet. "In God's name,
please honor this house."

"I'm not here to visit you."

"Who then?"

"There is a new-moon new-man planted near here,
spending the lightness of his humility
like blossoms on the ground.
Where is Hilal?"

"I haven't seen him for days.
He must be out with the mules and the horses."

Muhammed runs to the stable. It's dark,
and the stench of manure is strong,
but all that vanishes when Friendship enters.

Miracles don't cause faith, but rather
the scent of kindredness that unites people.

Miracles overwhelm unbelief.

Faith grows from Friendship.

With the familiar fragrance, Hilal wakes up.
How could such a thing be in a stable?

Through the legs of the horses he sees
the robes of Muhammed! He comes crawling out
from the dark corner and lays his cheek
on Muhammed's feet. Muhammed puts his cheek
on Hilal's and kisses his head and face.

"How hidden can one be!
Are you better? How are you?"
                                        HOW!

A man sits and eats damp clay for moisture.
How is it with him when a flood of fresh
prophetic rainwater suddenly rides him along?

How is it when a blind, filthy dog wakes up,
and finds that he's a lion, and not
a lion such as could be killed,
but a spirit-lion who shatters sword
and javelin with just his presence?

How would that feel? A man crawls for years
on his stomach with his eyes closed.
Then one moment he opens his eyes,
and he's in a garden. It's spring.

How is it to be free of HOW,
loose in howlessness?

Howlers sit waiting around your table.
Throw them a bone!

This suggestion: wash before going to the watertank.
The waters there have grace enough to clean
and give you peace, but wash yourself
of how's before you go.

Wash off all wonderings-why
and workings-out-however.
Don't take those with you
to the big watertank.

Husam! Bats don't bother Husamuddin.
He's an expert on sunlight!

He's written about the new moon, Hilal.
Now he'll write about the full moon, the Sheikh.
New moon and full moon are the same.

A new moon teaches gradualness
and deliberation and how one gives birth
to oneself slowly. Patience with small details
makes perfect a large work, like the universe.

What nine months of attention does for an embryo
forty early mornings will do
for your gradually growing wholeness.

You don't win here with loud publicity.
Union comes of not-being.

These birds do not learn to fly
until they *lose* their feathers!

Humble living does not diminish. It fills.
Going back to a simpler self gives wisdom.

When a man makes up a story for his child,
he becomes a father and a child
together, listening.

Some souls flow like clear water.
They pour into our veins
and feel like wine.

I give in to that. I fall flat.
We can sail this boat lying down!

A craftsman pulled a reed from the reedbed,
cut holes in it, and called it a human being.

Since then, it's been wailing a tender agony
of parting, never mentioning the skill
that gave it life as a flute.

They say I tell the truth.
Then they ask me
to do a puppet show
of myself in the bazaar.

I'm not something to sell.
I have already been bought!

Don't try to hold on to this.
                    You'll lose it.
Don't pull the curtain.
                It will end.
This moment with all of us here
                        is paradise,
but don't try to leave this way.
                    You'll ruin it.

Leave, with your scholarship
and your philosophies.

Even if you reduced them
to a single hair's breadth,

there'd be no room here for those,
as now the dawn comes up.

In the wholeness of the sun,
it's an impudence to light lamps.

Friend, this talking about you
keeps me from enjoying
your presence.

Your face disappears
in its own shining.

When I think of your lips,
I can't come near.

Remembering other times
prevents this now.

You that hand me this cup,
you are my soul and my loving.

Whatever enthusiasm I've had,
you are those, and any success
is yours. Clap for yourself!
These are your hands.

Now

Now that you live here in my chest,
anywhere we sit is a mountaintop.

And those other images,
which have enchanted people
like porcelain dolls from China,
which have made men and women weep
for centuries, those have changed now.

What used to be pain is a lovely bench
where we can rest under the roses.

A left hand has become a right.
A dark wall, a window.

A cushion in a shoe heel,
the leader of the community!

Now silence. What we say
is deadly to some
and nourishing to others.

What we say is a ripe fig,
but not every bird that lights
eats figs.

The Lame Goat

You've seen a herd of goats
going down to the water.

The lame and dreamy goat
brings up the rear.

There are worried faces about that one,
but now they're laughing,

because look, as they return,
that goat is leading!

There are many different kinds of knowing.
The lame goat's kind is a branch
that traces back to the roots of presence.

Learn from the lame goat,
and lead the herd home.

SAADI: A Wife and a Wasp's Nest

SHAIKH MUSLIHUDDIN SAADI

*B**eloved ones of God,*

My subject today is Saadi, the great Sufi poet of Persia. In point of fact, all the poets of Persia were Sufi poets. Their point of view is recognized as the Sufi point of view. And not only the poets of Persia, but also the poets of India.

The works of Saadi have been considered in the East simple, and at the same time educational, and at the same time uplifting.

The beauty of the works of Saadi is that they begin with the education of children. His "Carima" is taught to children of nine, ten or eleven, and at the same time it is not just a legend or amusing story: it is like a seed sown in the heart of the child of that age, that in time it may flourish and bring forth fruits of good thought and imagination. "Carima" is a thanksgiving poem; in it the first lesson Saadi gives is to learn how to be grateful, how to express gratitude, how to appreciate.

And so he teaches the lesson of gratefulness and appreciation for all in the world, for the kindness and love of mother and father, and of friend and companion, by teaching first the gratefulness to God for all the blessings and benefits man receives. Saadi begins in "Carima" by saying: "O Lord, most merciful, I ask Thy forgiveness, for I am limited and in this life of limitation I am always apt to make errors."

He teaches in the first lesson for mankind to recognize his limited condition, and that this limitedness makes him subject to error. And at the same time he suggests the innermost desire of every soul to rise above the limitations and keep from error, to seek divine love and ask pardon, and to appreciate all the blessings he receives in life, in order to rise towards that ideal stage of the humane man. And as we see life today it seems this is the very thing which is lacking.

When children grow up without that tendency of appreciation, they often cannot understand what their mother has done for them, what their father has done for them, what their duty is to their kind friends, to elderly people, to their teacher. And when they grow without developing that gratefulness in their nature, the egoistic nature which naturally develops becomes terrible. A boy who does not appreciate in his childhood all that his mother has done for him, cannot then learn to be tender and gentle to his wife, for his first lesson he has learned from his mother.

Everything that by nature springs up has to be refined, and in its fulfillment it has to become perfect. In human nature there is a self-asserting tendency from childhood. Most pronounced in the nature of the child is "I," and everything that he possesses he says "my." And if that is not changed, if the same attitude remains, when that child grows older he becomes hard on those around him, for his "I" and what he calls "my" become difficult for all those around him.

The whole religious, spiritual and philosophical teaching leads us toward the development of the personality. There is something that is made by nature in man, but there is something that the man himself has to make. Man is born as man, but man develops to become humane. And if man remains only man as he is born, and the other qualities with which he is born remain undeveloped, and without being made refined, then he does not fulfil the object of life.

All the great teachers and masters of this world who have come from time to time, and whom we recognize as saints and sages, masters, teachers and inspired helpers: it is not always the philosophy they taught man, it is not always the dogmas or the form of religion they gave; what has been of the greatest importance is their personality, is their person.

The teachings of Buddha are held by many millions— but more than his teachings, the life he lived and the wisdom he expressed in his life, for there is the fulfill-ment. Man is born with a purpose, and that purpose is fulfilled in the refinement of his personality. This unrefined nature of the ego, when developed through life, has an effect like the sting of a thorn. Wherever, whoever, whatever it touches, it causes some harm or disturbance, some destruction.

And so personalities in human beings, when they are not refined, and they have before them all temptations, all things that attract them, things they like and admire and wish to have—then they go against the conflicting activities of life, they rub up against everything like a thorn tearing it in pieces. And what happens? No doubt when thorns rub against thorns they crush one another and they feel it less. But when thorns rub against flowers, they tear them to pieces.

If you will ask individuals in this world, in all walks of life, " Tell me, what is your difficulty in life?," perhaps they will tell you that they lack wealth or power or position. But mostly the complaint will be that they are in some way or other hurt by others: by friend or parent or child, lifemate or neighbor or co-worker. They are disturbed or troubled and in difficulty by this thorn-like influence from morning to evening touching them and scratching them. And yet man does not seem to think deeply on this subject. Life is blinding, and it keeps man busy and engaged finding fault with others. He does not find the thorn in himself, he always sees the thorn in others.

Saadi, in simple language, has tried to give man a helping hand towards the development in his personality of that flowerlike quality; to train this personality, which was made to be a flower, and to help. His whole life's work has been to explain to man how life can turn into a flower. He has called his books "Gulistan," which means a flower bed or rose garden; and "Bustan," a place of all sorts of fragrances, a place of fragrance.

In this he has tried to explain to man how the heart can be turned into a flower. In reality it is a flower, it is made to be a flower. It is made to spread its perfume. If only you trained it and tended it, it would show the delicacy and beauty and fragrance of a flower; and that is the purpose of your life.

There is no mystification in Saadi's poetry. It is full of wit and intelligence, and at the same time original. And the most wonderful thing that one sees in the poetry of Saadi is his humorous trend of mind. He is ready to look at the funny side of things and to amuse himself and enjoy. And how few of us in this world know what real, true mirth means—humor that is not vulgarized, not abused. It shows the rhythm and tune of the soul.

Without humor, life is dull and depressing. Humor is the reflection of that divine life and sun which makes life like the day. And a person who reflects divine wisdom and divine joy adds to the expression of his thought when he expresses his ideas with mirth.

One day Saadi was sitting in a bookseller's shop, where his books were sold. The bookseller was absent, and someone came in and asked for one of Saadi's books, not knowing that he was speaking to Saadi himself. Saadi asked, "What do you like about Saadi's books?" He replied, "O, he is a funny fellow." Whereupon Saadi made him a present of the book, and when he wished to pay for it, said, "No, I am Saadi, and when you called me a funny fellow, you gave me all the reward I wish."

He wanted life to be joyous. Spirituality is not in a long face and deep sigh. No doubt there are moments when you will sympathize with the troubles of others. There are moments that move you to tears, and there are times when you must just close your lips. But there are other moments when you can see the joyous side of life and enjoy its beauties. Man is not born into this world for depression and unhappiness. His very being is happiness; depression is something unnatural. By this I do not mean to say that sorrow is a sin or suffering always avoidable.

We all have to experience both in life, to accomplish the purpose of life. We cannot always be smiling. There is no spiritual evolution in ignoring either side of life. Spirituality is in every side of life. As long as one is not bound, it is no sin to stand in the midst of life. Man

need not go into the forest, away from all people, to
show his goodness and virtue. Of what use is his good-
ness and virtue if he buries himself in the forest? It is
right in the midst of life that we have to develop and
express all that is beautiful and perfect and divine in our
souls.

Saadi has expressed a wonderful thought in his work
called the "Gulistan," and in simple words. He says,
"Every soul was meant for a certain purpose, and the
light of that purpose was kindled in that soul." It is one
little verse, but it is a book in itself. What does this
suggest to us? That this whole universe is like one
symphony, and all souls are as different notes. Their
activities are according to the rhythm of this symphony,
and their life is purposed to perfect this symphony.

People are anxious to do something, and wait for years
and years, unhappy, in despair, waiting for that
moment to come. It shows that the soul knows in its
subconsciousness that there is a note to strike, and the
moment when it shall strike that note that soul shall be
satisfied. And yet it does not know what note it is, nor
when it shall be struck.

What is life? And what keeps us living in this world of
limitation, world of continual changes, world full of
falsehood, and world full of suffering and trouble? If
there is anything in this world that keeps us alive, it is
hope. Hope, the honey of life.

There is not one soul in this world who says, "Now, I
am satisfied; I have no further desire." In everyone,
whatever be the position in life, someone very rich or
one very poor, one full of life and the other ill, in all
conditions, man is continually yearning and waiting for
something to come. He does not know what, but he is
waiting.

The real explanation of life is waiting, waiting for something. And what is it that man awaits? It is the fulfillment of the purpose of life, which comes when the soul strikes that note, that note which is meant to be his note. And this he seeks, whether in the outer plane or the inner plane. Man has not fulfilled his life's purpose until he has struck that note which is his note. And the greatest tragedy in life is the obscurity of purpose. When purpose is not clear, man suffers, he cannot breathe. He knows not what is the purpose, what he must do.

This life will present to him things that will interest him for the moment, but the moment he possesses that thing he will say, "No this is not it, it is something else." So man goes on, in an illusion, constantly seeking, and yet not knowing what he seeks. Blessed is he who knows his life's purpose, for that is the first step to fulfillment.

And how are we to know our life's purpose? Can anybody tell us? No. No one can tell us. For life in its very nature is self-revealing, and it is our own fault if we are not open to that revelation which life offers to us. It is not the fault of life, because the very nature of life is revealing. Man is the offspring of nature, therefore his purpose is in nature. But the artificiality of life brings obscurity, which prevents him from arriving at that knowledge which may be called the revelation of one's own soul.

And if you ask me how one should proceed, I would advise you to study every object, whether false or true, which holds and attracts you, to which you are outwardly attracted and also inwardly attracted. And do not be doubting and suspicious. What Christ taught from morning until night was faith, but the interpretation of this word is not made clear. People have said faith in priest, in church, or in sect. That is not the meaning.

The true meaning of faith is trust in one's self. A person came to me and said, "I wish to follow your ideas, will you receive me? Will you have me follow you?" I said, "Yes, but will you tell me if you have faith?" This person looked perplexed for a moment; then he said, "Well, I have faith in you." I asked, "Have you faith in yourself?" He said, "Well, I am not sure." I said, "Your faith in me would be of no use to me; what I need is your faith in you."

Friends, what we must learn in life, is first to trust ourselves. This wobbling tendency of mind—shall I or shall I not; whether it is good or it is bad—this keeps man in confusion. And for years he may have the best intentions, but he will linger in the same place. He will not advance, for his own confusion will paralyze his legs. He will think he is going on, but he will be stepping in the same place where he is standing.

Man must have initiative. And this is the word from which comes initiation. Who is the initiate? The brave, the courageous. Who is brave and courageous? The one who trusts himself. Only his trust in himself will be of any use to himself or others.

People say, "Those of simple faith and trust suffer much and come to failure." I will say no, because what is gained is so much more than what is lost. In order to strengthen the trust, one has to meet with some failures. I would rather trust and be badly treated, than to distrust. The strength that faith and trust gives is the divine strength. The man who trusts his fellow creatures inspires trust in others. He can so develop that he will turn the untrustworthy into the trustworthy. With sufficient trust in his heart, he can develop the power to do this.

I always remember the blessing I received from my holy Master, my Teacher. It was, "May your faith be strengthened." Being young, I wondered that he said nothing about happiness, long life or prosperity. I have now learned to understand the meaning of that blessing, and understand it better every day. All the blessings that man attains in life, all that is in heaven and earth, become the possession of man when his faith is strengthened.

We read every day in the scriptures of "faith," but how little we think of it, and how many people at the present moment are beginning to laugh at it. Faith they give no attention to. It is something that conveys nothing to them. It is so simple and yet so complex. It is a miracle. It is a wonder. All our weakness, all our failure, all our limitation, all our suffering, comes from lack of that substance which is faith. All success, happiness, and advance, all that is achieved, the credit is due to faith.

The works of Saadi from the beginning teach the first lesson of faith; of understanding that we are not here in this world in vain, to waste our lives. We are here for a purpose, and each one of us for a particular purpose. Each one of us makes an atom of this universe, and completes the symphony; and when we do not strike our note, it means that note lacking in the symphony of the whole. And when we do not fulfil our life's purpose in this way, for which we are created, we are not living right—and therefore we are not happy.

Our happiness depends on living right, and right living depends on striking that note; and the realization of that purpose is in the book of our heart. Open that book and look at it. All meditation, all concentration

and contemplation is only to open this book, to focus
our mind, and to see what purpose there is in our life.
And no sooner do we see that our ultimate goal and our
life's object and happiness, our true health and well-
being and our real wealth and welfare, are in the fulfill-
ment of our purpose, then the whole trend of life will
change.

Translator's Introduction
Saadi: A Wife and a Wasp's Nest

Saadi was born in Shiraz around 1200 and died there in 1292. His long life is usually described by Persian literary biographers as having divided into three distinct parts. The first twenty-five years in education, the next thirty in far-ranging travels, and the last thirty in writing books and on dervish retreat. He is known as Sheikh Saadi, so there was undoubtedly a community of students around him in the last period.

He is most well-known for two collections of stories and moral sayings, The *Gulistan* (Rose Garden) and the *Bustan* (Kitchen Garden). Saadi's tone is more wry and didactic than the other poets in this anthology. He does not work on the edge of mystical trance. He is realistic, solidly set in the region of behavior: what to do with a wasps' nest in, or near, the house, and a sentimental wife who doesn't want them disturbed. The world he inhabits is more specific than ecstatic. The trickster Nasruddin presides over these tales more than Khidr, the Guide of souls. There is guidance here, but given in an amused tone. Saadi was sitting near a bookseller's stall once when a man approached and asked for a book by Saadi. "What do you like about this author?" asked Saadi, unrecognized. "Oh, he's a funny man!" Pleased with that evaluation, the poet gave him the book for free.

These selections were done almost exclusively from James Ross' early nineteenth century translations. Ross was a military surgeon stationed near Calcutta. Like Stephenson on Sanai and Clarke on Hafiz, Ross was an English military man stationed in India and a scholar of poetry, an exotic combination now, but evidently not that unusual during the Raj. Coming from the discipline and enthusiasm of the British school system, they each pursued diligently through the Indian heat their stubborn and demanding love of Persian mystical poetry. The difficulties of their efforts may perhaps be gauged by the fact that Dr. Ross once returned on furlough to England, and the voyage home took eleven months! I salute

these dogged ancestors with enormous gratitude: Major J.
Stephenson of the Indian Medical Service, Lieutenant
Colonel H. Wilberforce Clarke of the Bengal Lancers, and
Senior Surgeon with the 18th Regiment, Native Infantry,
Dinejapur, James Ross.

I heard of a man once who learned how it was to be married and a householder. Wasps built a nest under his roof, but his wife would not allow him to dispose of them. "Poor things, they need their little home." Then one day they stung her by the gate and in the lane. She cried for help, and the husband replied, "You said the poor wasps should not be hurt." Be careful with your pity. Kindliness on the nightwatch only brings out more thieves, and then nobody gets any rest.

A certain man, completely naked and without any
provisions whatsoever, joined us on our pilgrimage to
Mecca. He explained himself, "I am not lord over any-
one, nor is anyone lord over me. I have no mount, and
I carry no baggage. I do not think of past triumphs or
future sorrows. I breathe the pure freedom of my
simple life." A gentleman riding on a camel commented,
"You dervish, you'll never make it across the desert.
Return to town." But the naked man did make it on
foot to the first night's oasis, whereas the rich man on
the camel died suddenly in his sleep that same night.
And then there's the instance of the one who sat up all
one night weeping by a sick friend's bed and died the
next day, while the invalid recovered. Many fleet
horses expire on the road, as the lame donkey plods
home.

A powerful, but moody, man struck a dervish on the head with a stone. The dervish picked up the stone and kept it for years, until the man fell into disfavor and was put in a dungeon. The dervish went there and threw the stone through the bars. "Why did you do that?" "Years ago you hit me with that very stone." "But why have you waited till now?" "I respected your high station, but now I see no reason to."

A man had a beautiful wife who died, but the mother-in-law continued to live in the house, claiming the rights of the dowry. Some friends came to comfort him and took him aside. "How it is since your dear friend died?" He answered, "The absence of my wife is not so hard to endure as the presence of her mother. They plucked the rose away from the thorn. They emptied out the treasure and left me the snake."

They put a crow in the cage with a parrot, and both were annoyed. "Where did they find such a hideous creature!" screamed the parrot. And the crow was thinking, "What sin did I commit to deserve this conceited, babbling fool?" I tell this little story to show that the snobbery scholars feel toward uneducated people is *exactly* reciprocated. One time a strict ascetic fell in with a company of wandering poets. "Welcome, dear holy man," began a charming minstrel from Balkh. "I can see that you disapprove of us, but please don't frown. You already look offensive enough."

I asked a scholar the meaning of the tradition which says, "Your most subtle and deadly adversary is the sexual energy in your loins." "The reason is this," he answered. "Any ordinary enemy that you treat politely will begin to be your friend, except that lust-energy. The more you indulge and placate that, the more powerfully it drags you both down. Strong discipline needs to be brought forward to stop that bully from killing you."

A dervish's wife was pregnant, her term nearly
completed. He prayed, "If God will give me a son, I'll
distribute all I have to the poor, except for this ragged
robe I'm wearing." And it happened. The wife gave
birth to a son, and the dervish gave a great entertain-
ment to celebrate the acknowledgement of his vow.
Several years after, I was returning from Syria when I
passed a friend's house and asked about the dervish.
"He's in jail." "How did that happen?" "His son got
drunk, killed a man in a fight, and fled the city. When
that happens, as you know, the father is put in chains."
So there he sits with an iron collar on his neck, and he
brought it on himself with his praying! It would have
been better if the child had been a snake, rather than
this ungrateful son who won't accept the outcome of
his actions.

Having tired of the company of my friends in
Damascus, I went out on retreat into the wilderness
around Jerusalem, where a band of Frankish workers
abducted me and made me dig ditches. Presently, one of
the ruling class of Aleppo, an old acquaintance, saw me
there and took pity and redeemed me from slavery with
ten dinars. He took me back to Aleppo and gave me his
daughter in marriage, who soon turned out to be a
witch with a scorching tongue, the worst fate that can
happen! "Have you heard," I asked him, "of the kind
man who saved a sheep from a wolf and that night slit
its throat in the shed?"

In Baghdad an old man gave his daughter in marriage
to a shoemaker. On the wedding night the cobbler in
his passion bit the girl's lip so hard that it bled. The next
morning the father saw the cut and said to the man,
"Must your teeth chew my daughter like they do the
shoe leather? Don't let this be a habit! I am not joking.
When a violent quirk takes hold in sexual pleasure, only
death can uproot it."

The King of Arabia heard the story of Majnun's love for Laila and called him to his court. "What have you seen in her that makes you so distracted that you always cut your hand when you peel an orange?" "Many have asked that, but if you could see her...." The king searched and brought Laila forward. She was thin and dark, less appealing than the least of his harem girls. "Ah," said Majnun, "you must see her through the wicket of *my* eyes. There is a great difference between holding a little salt in your hand and putting it on a wound."

A certain man entered the city with a caravan from the south. He had his hair plaited, and he claimed to be a direct descendent of Ali just returning from Mecca. He presented the king with an elaborately wrought *qasida*, a poem praising the king, who was greatly impressed. He gave the holy poet gifts and treated him with lavish respect. Then one of the courtiers returned from a sea voyage and said, "I saw this man north of here at Bosra during the annual festival. He could not have been on hajj." And another remembered, "Yes! His father was a Christian from Malta. He's no descendent of Ali." They discovered the poem in the works of Anwari. The king ordered him to be brought. "Before I banish you, one question. Why did you lie so outrageously?"
"Sovereign of the Universe, I'll make one more speech, and if you find it false, I'll accept whatever punishment you say." "Proceed." "If a poor country man brings you a cup of buttermilk, it will be two-thirds water. If your servant brags of his adventures, you must expect that of world-travelers!" The king smiled. "I don't dispute these words." He gave the imposter traveling provisions, and they parted amicably.

Whoever advises a self-sufficient man needs advice.

This happened when I was young, as it must have to you. I had a friend with a voice like a flute and a face like silver. But something in his behavior, I forget what, irritated me, and I withdrew my affection. "You won't listen to me. Go and follow your own way." As he left, I heard him say, "If a bat doesn't relish the sun's company, can the sun diminish his brilliance?" I felt immediately how I didn't want him to go, but I didn't call him back. He wandered for years, returning finally with his flute-voice cracked and his Joseph-face bearded. "You left a sleek antelope. You return surly like an old leopard." This is the story of youth ending. There's no controlling how that goes. "What became of your beauty?" "It put on black, this beard, to mourn its departure."

One night I was thinking of what I had done in my fifty
years, and weeping at the waste. Every moment a
breath goes out that will never return. The fascinating
drowse of the morning keeps the traveler from
traveling. Many have plans for a home that they leave
the building of to the next generation. I saw that my
postponing could last for thousands of years. I resolved
to make a retreat into silence, and I did. But an old
friend came to my secret holy place, and demanded that
I sit up all night with him telling stories. "The warrior
Ali doesn't leave his sword in the scabbard, and likewise
Saadi, the great talker, must talk!" It was the first of
April, and the garden was being so garrulous and
generous all around that I gave in. At dawn, I said, "I
wish these flowers and this conversation could keep
blooming forever." And as I said it, the idea came for a
book that would be called *The Flower Garden*, a place
where roses would open all through the year.

HAFIZ: A Dazzling Turn

KHWAJA SHAMSUDDIN MOHAMMED HAFIZ

*B*eloved ones of God,

My address today is on the subject of Hafiz, whose name is well known to everyone interested in the poetry of Persia because among the Persian poets Hafiz stands unique in his expression, in his depth of thought, in the excellence of his symbolical expression of certain thoughts and philosophy.

There was a time when a deep thinker and a free thinker had great difficulty in expressing his thoughts, and that time has not altogether ceased. But at the same time, in some ways there seems to be much more freedom of expression in this age than in ancient times. At that time, anyone who expressed his thought freely about life and its hidden law—about soul, God, creation and manifestation—met with great difficulty.

The difficulty was that the religious authorities of all kinds governed, and under the religious reign the principles of the exoteric religion reigned. And therefore those who attained by the esoteric side of

philosophy always had difficulty in telling it to the
people. Many were persecuted; they were stoned, they
were flayed, they were put to death. All sorts of punish-
ment were inflicted upon them, and in this way the
progress of humanity was retarded. Today we do not
see this. At the same time, the limited attitude of the
human mind on religious and philosophical questions is
to be found in all ages.

The Sufis, who found by the help of meditation the
source of knowledge in their own hearts, for them it
was very difficult to give to the world in plain words
what little they could explain of the truth. It is true that
the truth cannot be spoken in words; but at the same
time, those gifted with poetic and prophetic expression
have always had that inclination and tendency of
expressing what their souls experienced.

Hafiz found a way of expressing the experience of his
soul and his philosophies in verse. For the soul enjoys
expressing itself in verse because the soul itself is music,
and when it is experiencing the realization of divine
truth the tendency of the soul is to express itself in
poetry. Hafiz therefore expressed his soul in poetry.
And what poetry! Poetry full of light and shade, line
and color, and poetry full of feeling. No poetry in the
world can be compared to that of Hafiz in its delicacy.

Only the fine soul, who has the finest perception of
light and shade expressed in words, can grasp the mean-
ing of the illumination of the soul. At the same time, the
words of Hafiz have won every heart that listens. Even
if they do not wholly understand it, the phrase, rhythm,
charm and beauty of expression win them. It is the
same style that Solomon adopted, but it was spoken in
the language of the time.

Hafiz spoke in the language which was most appropriate and most suitable to poetry. The Persian language is considered in the East the most delicious language, a language which stands supreme to all Eastern languages in poetry. It is soft, and its expression is tender. It is expressive. Every object has perhaps ten names for the poet to choose from. Every little thought can be expressed in perhaps twenty different ways, and the poet has that freedom of choice. And therefore the Persian language and Persian poetry both are rich in expression.

The mission of Hafiz was to express, to a fanatically-inclined religious world, the presence of God, which is not to be found only in heaven, but to be found here on earth.

Very often religious belief in God and in the hereafter has kept man sleeping, waiting for that hour and that day to come when he will be face to face with his Lord, and he is certain that that day will not come before he is dead. And therefore he awaits his death in the hope that in the hereafter he will see God, for heaven alone is the place where God is to be found, there is no other place were God will be found. And that there is only a certain place which is a sacred place of worship, that is, the church, and that anywhere else God was not to be found.

The mission of Hafiz was to take away this idea and to make man conscious of the heaven by his side, and to tell man that all he expects in the hereafter as a reward, could be had here, if he lived a fuller life.

The same ideal which one sees in all religions, which Jesus Christ taught, saying, "God is love"—that was the main idea of Hafiz, the idea that he has expressed from morning to night in the *Divan*. If there is anything divine in man, it is love. If God is to be found anywhere, it is in man's heart, which is love, and if the love element is awakened in the heart then God is made alive, so to speak, and is born in one's self.

But at the same time Hafiz has shown in his poetry the key to this, and that key is appreciation of beauty in all forms. Beauty is not always in an object or in a person. Beauty depends upon one's attitude towards life, how one looks at it; and its effect depends upon our power of appreciation. The very same music or poetry or painting will touch one person so that he feels its beauty to the very depth of his being, and perhaps there is another person who looks at it, but he does not see it.

The whole manifestation has its beauty: sometimes the beauty is manifest to you, sometimes you have to look for it. There comes a good person; we are always charmed by the beauty of goodness. There comes another person who looks bad. But at the same time good is somewhere hidden in him, if we would look for it, if we have the desire to draw it out. The look of bad is not always in objects and persons, but in our looking.

The whole trend of the poetry of Hafiz is to awaken that appreciation of beauty and love of beauty, which is the only condition through which to experience that bliss for which our life is purposed. Someone asked a Sufi the reason for this whole creation, and he answered, "God, Whose being is love itself, had desire to experience the nature of His own being, and in order to experience it, He had to manifest Himself."

God Himself and His manifestation, the soul and God: this dual aspect can be seen in all forms of nature—in the sun and the moon; in night and day; in male and female; in positive and negative; and in all things of opposite characters—in order that this love principle, itself the original and the only principle at the back of the whole manifestation, may have the scope of its full play. And therefore the fulfillment of the purpose of life is in the full expression of the love principle.

Very often people by learning philosophy, and by looking at this world with a pessimistic thought, have renounced the world and have called it material and false; and have left this world and have gone to the forest or desert or cave, and have taught the principle of self-denial and self-abnegation and renunciation. That was not the way of Hafiz.

He said it is like journeying over the sea and coming to a new port, and before landing one becomes frightened, saying, "But I shall perhaps be attacked by the people; or the place will attract me so much that I will not be able to go back where I have come from." But he does not know why he has taken that journey. He has not taken the journey to go back without landing.

The attitude of Hafiz is to land there. Risk it. If it is an attractive place, he is ready to be won. If it will crush him, he is ready to be crushed. This is a daring attitude. Not running away from this false world, but in this false world to discover glimpses of the true. And in this maze to find God's purpose.

Besides this, there is another great revelation which Hafiz has brought before humanity in a most beautiful form. Now, there are many people in this world who have once believed in God, in His mercy and compassion, in His love and forgiveness, but after having suffered, after seeing catastrophes and injustice, have given up belief. Many people after great sorrow and suffering have given up religion.

The reason is that the religion they have followed has taught them God as goodness, God as judge. Well then, they ask from a judge justice. Justice to satisfy their

own ideas. They think their standard of justice is God's.
They look for goodness as they understand it. And
therefore there comes a time of struggle in their hearts.
They do not see justice, because they are looking from
their own point of view. They are looking for goodness,
kindness and mercy from their own point of view. And
there are many conditions which make them think
there is no justice, that there is no such thing as a
forgiving element.

But the way of Hafiz is different. There is hardly the
name of God to be found in the *Divan*. He does not give
that belief of God, the just and good. His God is his
Beloved, to whom he has surrendered in perfect love
and devotion, and everything coming from the Beloved
is taken by him with love and devotion as the reward.
He prefers poison coming from the hand of the Beloved
to nectar from another. He prefers death to life if it is
the wish of the Beloved.

But you may say, "Is it fair?" There is no question of
fairness where there is love. Love stands above law.
Law is beneath love, law is born of love. The mistake in
this day is that we keep law higher than love. We do
not see that the divine principle, which is love, stands
above law. Man makes God a judge who is bound by
law; who cannot do His will, but has to do according to
what is written in His book.

God is not justice. Justice is His nature, but love is
predominant. People give such importance to one's
actions and their results. They do not know that above
action and result is a law which can consume the fire of
hell, which can dominate if the whole world were being
drowned in the flood of destruction—that the love
power is greater than any other.

Think of the hen when she takes care of her little ones.

If they were threatened with danger, though it were a horse or an elephant, she would fight, because the love principle is predominant. A kind mother is ready to forgive when her son comes with his head bowed and says, "Mother, I have been foolish, I have not listened to you; I have been insolent, I am sorry." She is ready to understand. She is ready to forgive. So we see mercy and compassion going out as love, a stream of love which can purify all the evil actions of years.

Then if a human being can actually forgive, can not God forgive? Many of the dogmatic religions have taken away the love element which is predominant, which makes God sovereign. And they make a God who is limited, who is bound by the book, and who cannot show his compassion. If God were so limited He could not be just. An individual would be better, because an individual can forgive.

Hafiz gives a picture of human nature: hate, jealousy, love, kindness, vanity; the play of friendly impulse, the play of pride: all aspects of life. Hafiz is not a poet, he is a painter. He has made a picture of the different aspects of life. Every verse is a picture. And in every picture, whatever be its color—vanity, pride or conceit; love, mercy or compassion—in all its garbs, he sees only one spirit, the spirit of the Beloved. And he shows his devotion, appreciation and love to all the manifestations of that one and the same Beloved.

There are many religions and beliefs where it is said that there will come a day when man will be able to communicate with God. But when will that day come? Life is so short, and our hearts so hungry. And if it does not come today perhaps it will not come at all. Therefore the only thing that Hafiz has pointed out from beginning to end is this: "Do not wait for that day to come tomorrow. Communicate with the Beloved just now. He is before you here in the form of your friend and in the form of your enemy; with a bowl of poison or with a rose. Recognize it and know it, for this is the purpose of life."

Religions have made this like a journey of millions of miles. Hafiz has made it right at hand.

Man likes complexity. He does not want to take one step, it is more interesting to look forward to millions of steps. The man who is seeking the truth gets into a puzzle, and that puzzle interests him. He wants to go through that puzzle a thousand times more. Just like children: their whole interest is in running around. They do not want to see the door and go out, until they are very tired; and so with the grown-up people.

That is why the Mystics made the greatest truths a mystery, to be given to the few who were ready for it, and to let the others play, because it is the time for them to play.

As the love principle, according to the idea of the Sufis and according to the idea of all the Prophets and Knowers who have ever come to this world, is the first principle, so it is the last principle. There are different Yogas practised by the people of India, which are the Intellectual, Scientific, Philosophical and Moral paths to God; but the most desirable path to God that the Hindus have ever found, and which makes the whole life beautiful, is Bhakta Yoga, the path of devotion, because it is the natural path.

Man's inclination is love. If he is cold, it is because he is longing for love; if he is warm, it is because love is alive. If one is suffering from depression, is yearning or sorrowing, it is because the love principle is not alive.

143

The only life, the very source of inspiration, salvation and liberation, is love.

And among those great souls who have brought the message of God to humanity from time to time—Buddha, Krishna, Jesus Christ, Moses, Abraham, Zarathustra—they were well known as most learned men. And what they learned, they learned from the love principle. What they knew was compassion, forgiveness, sympathy, and tolerance; that attitude of appreciation; that opening of the heart to humanity. What they taught was love, a simple truth.

If religions seem complex, they have been added to. In every case what was brought by the Prophet was simple, and it was expressed in his personality and his life. And it is that influence that has remained for centuries after they have passed away. It is not the literature they have left—most of the literature is from their pupils. It is the simple truth shown in their personalities and their lives.

The error of this day and age is that we cannot understand the simple truth, the truth as manifested everywhere, instead of trying to find truth covered in a shell.

Hafiz at the same time teaches one to see the ultimate truth and the ultimate justice in one and the same thing, and it is God; that justice is not in related things, perfect justice is in totality. And he shows that the power behind manifestation is the love power, and it is by this power that this whole world was created. It is the love principle whether it works through God or man. And if that principle is at the back of the whole creation, then it is the same principle which helps man to fulfil the purpose of his life.

Translator's Introduction
Hafiz: A Dazzling Turn

For six centuries Hafiz has been scolded for inconsistency, for the giddy, slippery grace with which he skates from the profound to the comical to the passionate and then to a calm question, or almost anywhere. His poems have no coherence, they scream down the ages. There was even some talk of destroying his tomb because of his dissolute life (part of his inconsistency), yet the tomb area has been treated with great reverence as though the place had oracular powers. It is the custom when one goes there to open the *Divan* at random, and let it answer your question. Hafiz is a maze of ambiguities, which is to say he is himself, and completely unclassifiable. Many are unable to endure such authentic variety.

Others find him a startling truth-teller and consummate poet. Goethe, for example, perhaps the most complex artist in the Western world, loved Hafiz. He saw in him a "twin." Hafiz is as elusive as the Beloved he adores, the presence that is everywhere and nowhere, compellingly sensual and yet beyond, and within, the senses. Meher Baba (Hafiz was his favorite poet) said that "instead of the pearl inside Hafiz' poetry, most people see the oyster." The real meanings of Hafiz' poems, as one might expect, have been in great dispute, the sensual and the spiritual being so hopelessly tangled. It is this equilibrium that gives the famous jewel-like effect. Delicate and tough, a crafted danger, full of wit as well as abandon, Hafiz' lyric is one of the rare mysteries of world literature. The Persian ghazal form encourages the self-enclosure of each line and then great leaps between the lines, a perfect vehicle for his electric meanders.

Hafiz doesn't tell stories, and the poems rarely follow a "course." They hop and glide and burrow like no known animal. And always at the end there's the name-tag reference to "Hafiz." He took that pen-name for himself. It means "one who has memorized the entire *Qur'an*," or "the rememberer." He speaks of himself, or to himself, there at the end of the poem, with the effect that the poem is thrown into the Wit-

145

ness, a consciousness beyond the concerns of any Hafiz-personality.

With Hafiz the conventional divisions of awareness do not apply. Intellect, feeling, spiritual intuition, and the sensory grasp of moment and place all meld into a many-faceted, transparent whole. The jewel metaphor is cliche, but inescapable. Hafiz is a shape-shifter, and each poem plays in the risk of soul-change. Hafiz moves along the edge that so many have longed to discover, where soul-body and language-music distinctions dissolve, and a new life-form is born of their love.

Hafiz says, "How can you walk the true path, unless you step out of your own nature." This is the paradox he embodied. His poems are entirely natural, and yet they've stepped over the boundary into a madness of surrender. "O you, if you ever get lost enough to realize God, then you'll be dust on the feet of a Perfect Master." Becoming particles is Hafiz' image of this happening. On the forehead of a man, on the doorsill, or suspended in water, the granule of matter doesn't care where it is. Hafiz' poetry has that grainy feel, particulate in line and image and yet unified in the overall powder of his joy. Hafiz says, "A Master cannot only turn dust to gold but dust into an alchemy that changes everything to gold."

Consider this metaphor for his poetry. The sound of rain is language being used. Silence is an orchard when it's not raining, the ground moisture being quietly drawn up into the fruit trees. Then there's the Hafiz-place, in between silence and speaking, when it's quit raining, but a rain-like dripping continues in the orchard. His poetry is a peace so fine it keeps overflowing, as though from nowhere.

We know very little of his life. He was born in 1320 in Shiraz (southeast Iran). We know that he must have married and had a family. He mourns a wife and a son in the poems. He was invited to come to India as a court poet and also to Baghdad, but he remained in Shiraz.

A story has come down about the Indian offer. Hafiz was sent a hefty sum of money for travel expenses to India, but on the way to the port of Ormuz he met a friend who was destitute. Hafiz gave him all the money, but went on to the dock anyway. The crew thought him such a fine fellow that they agreed to let him travel for free. But then a storm came up, and Hafiz decided he didn't like the looks of the Indian Ocean. He wrote a poem and sent that to India in his stead. ("My Response to Your Offer"). Most of his life was spent near the town he loved so passionately, and its river, the Ruknabad. He seems to have made a meagre living as a copyist, as a teacher in the local college, and sometimes as a court poet. He was treated erratically, but overall fairly well, by a sundry, and quick, succession of rulers.

There is another interesting legendary account of a meeting between Hafiz and the most sinister figure of the era, the ferocious conqueror, Tamerlane, who swept south through Persia, killing seventy thousand people in Ispahan and entering Shiraz in December of 1387. He summoned the aging Hafiz, then sixty-seven, and confronted him with lines from one of the poems,

"If the young Turkish girl would accept my hand,
I'd give Bokara for the mole on her cheek,
                                        or Samarcand."

"With my bright sword," Tamerlane raged, "I have subjugated most of the known world, and yet you, a miserable wretch of a poet, would sell my native town and the seat of my government for the mole on a girl's cheek!"

"You're right," replied Hafiz bowing quickly. "It's by just such extravagant spending that I've come to the sorry position you find me in now."

The emperor was so delighted with Hafiz that he not only didn't punish him, but sent him away with a gift. Hafiz died and was buried in Shiraz in 1389.

Hafiz put together a collection of poetry in 1369, but no copies of that text remain. The earliest manuscript is a 1424 edition of a collection assembled by Hafiz' friend, Muhammed Gulandam, sometime after 1389.

The Quarry

It doesn't matter everyone's against me.
Being near you gives life.
Your absence, death.

A rose tears open from its center.
Will I go to sleep before you arrive?
Is longing all there is of love?

I want your knife more
than someone else's salve.

Let my head be the lance's target.
Don't hold back the horse,
and don't veer off!

Tie me close with the saddle strap
you use for small game.

When dust from your doorsill
is put on my head, they'll say, *Hafiz
has been crowned king*!

The Wild Deer

Wild deer, my friend
who traveled with me for years,
how is it now with us
crossing this vast plain separately?

Where we're going has not changed,
but without each other's company
the journey grows frightening.

I keep asking everywhere, "Who
can take the wild deer's place?
Khidr?" Is that Guide of guides
approaching! I hear footsteps.

But he separated us before, turning joy to grief.
Maybe he will change it back!

This time of year when God gives many gifts
the line came to me from the *Qur'an*,
where Muhammed cries out,
Don't leave me without children!

One day there was a rare spirit
sitting beside the road.

A traveler who was determined
to reach the great Simurgh bird
walked by.
              "Have you been given some sign
that sends you this way? No one has known,
till now, which way to head.

The sun put its bag of fire
in one of the scalepans.

What have you found to balance with that?"
The traveler had no answer.

Was it Khidr sitting beside the road asking?
Wait here till he comes again.
Sit by this spring and weep,
remembering those you've loved
that have died. Say your sadness
like a summer rain. Merge into the river
made of such tribute.

Hold tight to the stem of the rose you've been given.
Learn what such a friend is worth.
Write that in the margin and memorize it.

The strategy of this earth
is to pull companions apart.

But what I write here
does not flow from anything material.

This poetry mixes soul with mind.
It's a seed held in music
as in warm ground.

The fragrance you take in, listening,
comes from a peaceful presence, not
the wild deer who left me here alone!

Renunciation, and the Other Mystery

Tallest fir tree on the hillside,
softest lip, truest arrow,
opening the world's wine, you
say to this beggar:

"You give words light and eyes to wander,
how long will you be poor,

when following me you could play like a prince
and whisper to delicate ears?"

Then a warning from my ancestors comes,
"Don't listen to that voice!"
Allah give their souls peace.

I was walking through a garden,
red tulips and morning breeze.

Shall I honor this long line
of dead renunciates?

"Hafiz," comes the answer,
"you're not here to know *that* mystery.

Yours is a long kiss
on the cup circling by."

The Substance You Taste

The sky-wheel turns us into dawn
and fills creation again with color.

Let it be our weakness, this thirst-love
for the world, the sun coming up
like red-gold being poured!

The potter's wheel moves,
and shapes change quickly.

Let the jar I am becoming
turn to a wine cup.
Fill me with your love
for being awake.

I'm no hypocrite renunciate.
Call me this delicious substance
you taste when you create new beauty.

Be strong, Hafiz!
Work here inside time,
where we fail, catch hold
again, and climb.

Pour Me More

This is what the broke drunkard says.

Don't vex me with your contempt.
Old friends have certain rights, surely,
more rare than all the jewels you've stashed.

But your face, the wealth
that mirrors the sun and moon,
I can't say its value!

Don't scold me again. Whatever happened
was supposed to happen, wasn't it?

Don't you worry that my breath
may stain your white wool?

Pour me more of that from last night,
so I can forget how much I spent.

And Hafiz! I want to hear *your* songs.
They're the best, I swear it,
by the book inscribed
in your chest.

The Danger

Love seems easy in a circle of friends,
but it's difficult, difficult.

Morning air through the window, the taste of it,
with every moment camel bells leaving the caravanserai.

This is how we wake, with winespills
on the prayer rug, and even the tavernmaster
is loading up. My life has gone
from willfullness to disrepute,
and I won't conceal, either, the joy
that led me out toward laughter.

Mountainous ocean, a moon hidden behind clouds,
the terror of being drawn under.

How can someone with a light shoulder-pack
walking the beach know how a night sea-journey is?

Hafiz! Stay in the dangerous life that's yours.
There you'll meet the face
that dissolves fear.

The Zikr Circle

If love leads me to a musky, thick wine,
it must be what I need, not some austere hypocrisy.

If everyone in the world
advised against my loving you,
still I would.

One lives in the zikr circle
so that the round knot in the Beloved's hair
will be undone.

The beautiful bride of the world approaches,
but not to marry anyone!

Watch. One bride leaves,
as another comes.

The cypress, the tulip,
a line of gowns.

We are beggars here,
but don't ask what we're begging for!
Whatever it is shows in our faces.

So I said to tease the beauty, "My moon,
if we kissed, could I endure the love?"

"Hafiz," she laughed, "kiss on!
Your lips won't stain the moon."

The Wind of an Opening Rose

Last night's storm was a journey to the Beloved.
I surrender to that, the wind that
is my Friend, and my work.

Each night, the lightning flashes.
Every morning, a breeze.

Not in some protected place, but in the flood
of the heart's pumping, in the wind
of a rosebud's opening out,
that puts a small crown on each narcissus.

A tired hand collapses, exhausted,
that in the morning holds your hair again.

Peace comes when we are friends together,
remembering. Hafiz! Your honest desire
and your benevolence free the soul
to emerge as what it is.

A Daughter

You that drain the sky's clear cup,
wanderers of the imagination take a thousand years
to climb the path to you.

You are the eye and the lamp we use.
The sun and the moon? Just the simplest bits
left on the edge of your tray.

Praising you gave my mind a daughter
that now I bring you for a bride.

This poem be witness
I serve your kindness
like a slave.

Your Gestures

All I want is to be near you.
Praise God for this desire,
and let it intensify!

Priests and elders have a different view.
"Drunken sots," they call us lovers.

People with nothing that they want,
let them live their dim righteousness.

Darling, my soul, separated from you,
has no words but weeping.

The cypress tries to hold your gestures.
The moon, your look.

Hafiz does not much care anymore
for evening discourse or morning prayer,

when there's some small chance
you'll lean down to kiss.

Growing Tulips

Come back, tulip bed.
Thought smoothes to nothing
in the ocean of your dark mouth.

There is a physics of rain,
like elegant grieving.

I am alive, and yet not.
No great wonder.

A horseman drives forward to the barricade
with his reins tight.

During these one or two moments
when seeing the Beloved is possible,
what is the work of our lives?

The sweetest sleep begins at dawn,
but don't give in.
This chance may not come again!

Yesterday we didn't see each other. For me,
there's no purpose without those glances.

Helpless Hafiz! Keep using words,
for on this planet's surface
the only life-forms left

are those that grow
in the garden of these poems

Midnight Question

Near midnight, in disarray, you come asking,
"Is it still like this, my love,
when you're old?"

Who would refuse to answer?
The same was heard
before the creation of the universe,
"Am I not your Lord?"

Whatever's poured then must be drunk.
It may be pure soul, merely grape-wine,
or some combination, but say *Yes*,

as I have many times,
as we all once did in unison
outside time and space.

Never regret that answer!

Almost Empty

There is this matter
of the light in my eyes.

If you want to know the Friend,
don't expect elegant arguments!

Demand a blessing
from one who gives you joy.

Don't worry about livelihood or property.
Be a subsistence for your friends.
A sitar string drawn tight. A drum.

Be almost empty,
and the dreg-drinkers
will gather to taste.

I See

God's Light, I see
where and what that is,

but who drinks the dregs
in this wine-house?

I see the door,
and the prayer rug pointing its need,
and the archway.

I see who leads the way to Mecca.

I see the dignity of being a lover,
and the disgrace, and the playfulness.

I see the Kaaba.

I catch an eastwind fragrance every morning.

I see the point of unity in all creation,
with no why or how.

I see poor philosophy so far from reality.

I see that my fancy images fail.

But to whom shall I say what's left?

Don't come complaining
that Hafiz keeps claiming "I see,
I see," him and his crowd of God-lovers!

The Brim

You hide your face in the leaves,
and our eyes fill with rosewater,
sleepy as a narcissus opening.

You slip away in the garden seasons.
The purple violets, the white lily,
they change, and you hurry off.

Surface bubbles open their eyes,
and vanish. How different is
this world from those bubbles?

Your way with a body-cup
is to drain its love-wine.

Do that to us!

Ruknabad

Bring all the wine that's left!

When we're dead and wandering Paradise,
we won't find a place more beautiful
than this stream called Ruknabad,
by the gardens with their roses
in the town of Shiraz.

Allahu Akbar Pass

There's a difference between
the water of Khidr's spring, hidden
in the land of night, so difficult to reach,

and our water here, which comes down
from that narrow gorge in the mountains
to the north, from where on the road
you first see Shiraz, the pass called
Allahu Akbar, opening into praise!

My Response to Your Offer

How much delight would make
a broken back worth it?

If this dervish robe
could be exchanged for a wine cask,
now there's a deal!

Your crown as the King of India
is a circle of fear and suspicion.

Your jewels look fine in the mirror,
but their weight on the head's prohibitive.

Down in the Christian quarter
where they sell red wine, this prayer rug
won't bring enough for a cup.
So what's all the five-times business for?

Seawater seemed a bargain to cross
when your offer came.

Then a storm blew in,
and the ratio changed

between the Indian Ocean
and its pearls!

Lost

Send those who can be hired
to cry out in the lover's market:

"Lost! A wild daughter has been lost,
wearing a thin crown of foam
and a dark red dress.

She's dangerous!
She'll steal your mind,
and yet whoever finds her
can have my soul for a reward.

From wherever the shameless, blushing
grape of a girl has gone, bring her back
to the home of Hafiz, the poet."

Lost, a wild daughter
has been lost!

Shiraz

is the city
  inside the chest.
              Ruknabad,
the perfect river of perfection
              that threads through
                        its love, Shiraz.
Breezes blow from Ispahan
              and flowers from Jafarabad,
                        which is made of flowers,
yet both are only halfway
              to Shiraz. No need to import
                        Egyptian sweets. Shiraz
honey flows in Shiraz
              streets! East wind, what can you tell me
                        of my gypsy girl?
Is she happy?
              Is she well? Is Shiraz
                        a little tipsy tonight?
Don't wake me from my dream
              of being back there.
                        Hafiz must dissolve
in Shiraz to nourish her,
              as a mother's milk must,
                        her child.

Water Running Together

I will not deny what I desire.
My lips want your lips,
not a substitute.

I sleep with my head
on *this* doorsill,
not some other.

The grief of never having the peace of your presence
makes breath one long sigh.

When I am dead, open the grave
and watch a cloud of smoke rise around your feet,
smothered fire-fumes from my shroud.

Beloved, come near! A lover walks the meadow
looking for flowers. Every man and every woman
does this looking
like streams of water running everywhere together.

Show yourself here where the pitiful
sit and sing, where Hafiz' name
comes up, and brings tears.

The Signal to Begin

The glory of being young has come again!
The light wind, the basil.

The child that looks so wise
is running straight to you for a kiss!

The moon is a polo ball,
and also a polo stick!

Be helpful on the survival ark,
even though safety is not the point.

Every guest dies in the end. But for now,
Joseph has been released from prison!

Lift your wine in salute to freedom.
Don't be trapped, as others have,
by some quote from the *Qur'an*.

Abandon, says the rose,
and nightingales begin.

The Banquet

A gathering of good friends
talking quietly outdoors,

the banquet being served, a dry rosé
with a bite of kebab afterwards,

a wink from the one who pours,
Hafiz telling some story,

Hajji Qavam with his long laugh,
a full moon overhead,

the infinite mystery
of all this love.

If someone doesn't want the pleasure
of such an openhearted garden,

companionship, no, life itself,
must be against his rules!

Shhh

Don't ask me to describe
the taste of my poison.

At the end of years of wandering
I've chosen a Friend. Don't ask who!

I weep in the doorway.

Last night I heard you saying
what cannot be said.

Now you motion to me,
Don't tell.

The pain of being in my room alone
is really what cannot be spoken.

So, like Hafiz, I walk the love-road,
aware in a way that has no name.

A Shift in the Breeze

For a long time I've done tavern-work,
wearing the clothes of emptiness,
singing with those who feel joy,
but I didn't catch the subtle
truth-fragrance there,

so I'm leaving, leading
the sweet partridge of the Beloved along,
hoping to be ambushed.

I walk the open street like a breeze
in which the basil and the rose
rise and fall in prayer.

I'm trying to entice the arrow, your glance,
the threshold-kiss of majesty, to land here.

This is what I do: in a conventionally religious assembly,
I am "Hafiz," who knows the entire *Qur'an* by heart,
while in a tavern, I am the dreg-drinker.

Notice the dazzling turn
of that change!

That Moment in This

Remember the day we met,
the taste of that moment in this.

As the grief-river all around carries us away,
recall a garden with the gardener
quietly bending to work.

One who had secrets with Hafiz
that no longer has to keep them,
I remember that one now.

Taking a Riddle into the Tavern

For many years my heart wanted something from me,
not knowing that it was itself
what it wanted:

the desire for Jamshid's cup,
wherein all existence can be seen,
except for that chalice itself, that is.

There was a man beloved of God
who cried out to God, "Why
have you forsaken me?"

I took the riddle of this into a tavern
and asked the one who served.

He said, "Some secrets must be kept,
not told to the world at large.
The rosebud and the soul write mysteries
on their margins fold within fold.
Stay closed and wait."

"Your wine glass is the all-revealing cup!"

"Given before the creation."

"And what of that woman there
that I cannot forget?"

"Hafiz," said the tavernmaster, "this love
within you that speaks needs
some restraint!"

Remember

Dear friends, there's a Friend
inside the night. Remember.

And the duty of serving others,
remember that.

In the middle of any excitement,
when the musical moan of your lover
comes, remember.

As you put your hopeful hand on her waist,
as the face of one bringing you a song
lights with recognition, remember.

Just as your horse
is passing the others, remember.

As you sit down to take command,
remember Hafiz' face and the way of kindness.

As the empty threshold
does, remember.

The New Guide

Anyone who turns away ashamed
from the head of your street
will find no work to do
that does not bring disgust.

By the light of a sheikh
a pilgrim finds the Beloved.

Heart-lost, at life's end,
help us taste that wine!

The time of judging who's drunk
and who's sober, who's right or wrong,
who's closer to God or farther away,
all that's over!

This caravan is led instead
by a great delight, the simple joy
that sits with us. That is the grace.

Hafiz! It may be
that you've just poured a toast
that will wash love free
of all its pictures.

Inscriptions Over the Door

This, as the roses open, and now
as the nightingales open in their way,
these moments succeed one another.

Remember them all,
you time-worshipping sufis!

The law of repentence that's written on stone
shatters to powder when touched with a wineglass.

Bring joy into this audience hall
where everyone is self-sufficient,
or judged a drunk, or judged a judge,
or a bailiff or a witness.

This is not a courtroom anymore,
but a caravanserai with two doors.
We come and go. What does it matter
how the lintels are inscribed?

Pleasure brings difficulties.
Calamity comes with existing.

Don't try to figure what's real and what isn't.
Be happy. Every perfection dies.

A bird flies along and then settles on the road.
An arrow in even less time slides to the ground.

Hafiz, how can this pen's voice give thanks
that what it says passes into marks
made by someone else's hand?

The Wine of the Question

When my Friend lifts a glass in here,
the marketplace suddenly loses customers.

I kneel weeping,
Will you take my hand?

I float like a fish
waiting for your hook.

Most people see your eyes
and call for the police,

but Hafiz knows that the wine you offer
is the wine in the *Qur'an* of the question,
Am I not your Lord?

that you poured
as we said *Yes.*

Returning

The morning breeze comes back,
and from the southern desert
the lapwing returns.
The dove's soft song about roses,
I hear that again.

The tulip, who understands what the lily says,
went away, but now she's back.

With the sound of a bell,
strength and gentleness.

Hafiz broke his vow and damaged his heart,
but now, for no reason, his Friend forgives that,
and turns, and walks back up to his door.

A Note on These Translations

I have wavered in this collaborative work on Persian mystics between calling the outcome "versions" or "translations." *Translation* comes from the Latin "to bring across." A bridge between cultures and times. But *version* has "turning" in it, the phrasal gesture. Both have appeal and relevance. I opt now for "translations," hoping that ways are being shaped here to allow more spiritual exchange between the Middle East and the West. But it should never be thought that I work with the Persian. I have informants. The sources for this book are listed below. The titles, of course, are my own additions.

Volumes of poetry in Persian have titles. Individual poems do not. They are referred to usually by their numbering in whatever the standard edition is for the particular poet. It should also be said that I have chosen to place these densely rhymed Persian poems in the unrhymed tradition of American free verse, because that is our strongest, and most authentically spiritual, lineage, as well as the one I work most comfortably in. Saadi is the exception. The spontaneous burst of the untitled prose poem seemed more appropriate for his dour mirth.

Sources

Sanai

E.G.Browne, *Literary History of Persia*, Cambridge
University Press (Cambridge, 1964), Vol. II.

A Persian Forerunner of Dante, a pamphlet, tr. Reynold Nicholson, no publisher or place of publication listed, 1943.

Hakim Sanai, *The Walled Garden of Truth*, tr. David Pendlebury, E.P.Dutton (N.Y., 1976).

Hakim Sanai, *The First Book of the Hadiqatu L-Haqiqat*, or
The Enclosed Garden of Truth, tr. J. Stephenson, Samuel Weiser
reprint of 1908 Lahore edition.

Sources for specific poems:

SANAI: "Teaching Schoolboys," Stephenson, pp. 96-98;
"Streaming," Stephenson, pp. 66-70; "The Wild Rose of
Praise," Stephenson, p. 47; "Energetic Work," Stephenson, pp.
98-9; "The Good Darkness," Stephenson, pp. 38-40; "Naked in
the Bee-House," Stephenson, pp. 42-7; "Earthworm Guidance," Stephenson, pp. 59-62; "The Puzzle," Browne, p. 322;
"The Time Needed," Browne, pp. 321-2; "A Soul's Journey
Through the Time-Worlds," Nicholson's *A Persian Forerunner*
of Dante.

Attar

The Ilahi-nama of Attar, tr. John Andrew Boyle, Manchester
University Press (Manchester, 1976).

Eastern Poetry and Prose, tr. Reynold Nicholson, Cambridge
University Press (Cambridge, 1922).

The Conference of the Birds, tr. C.S.Nott, Shambhala Press
(Boulder, 1971).

Sources for specific poems:

ATTAR: "The Newborn," Boyle, pp.164-5; "Listening to the
Reed Flute," Boyle, pp.105-6; "The Street-Sweeper," Boyle,
p.341; "Looking for Your Own Face," Boyle, p.328; "Mysticism," Nicholson, p.138; "The Woman Who Dressed as a

Man," Boyle, pp. 30-45; The *Conference of the Birds* excerpts, Nott, pp. 114, 116, 119 and pp. 131-2.

Rumi

Discourses, tr. A.J.Arberry, Samuel Weiser (New York, 1961).

Mystical Poems of Rumi, tr. A.J.Arberry, Persian Heritage Series No.3, University of Chicago Press (Chicago, 1968).

Mystical Poems of Rumi, tr. A.J.Arberry, Persian Heritage Series No.23, Westview Press (Boulder, CO, 1979).

Badi-uz-Zaman Furuzanfar, *Kulliyat-e Shams*, 8 vols. Amir Kabir Press, (Teheran, 1957-66). Standard edition of Rumi's odes and quatrains.

John Moyne, unpublished literal translations, done from, and using the numbering of, the Furuzanfar edition listed above.

The Muthnawi of Jalaluddin Rumi, tr. Reynold Nicholson, 8 vols. Luzac & Co. (London, 1925-40).

Rudolf Otto, *Mysticism East & West*, Meridian Books (New York, 1957). Reprinted from the original Macmillan 1932 edition.

Sources for specific poems:

RUMI: "We Point to the New Moon," Furuzanfar #2114, John Moyne; "The Reed Flute," *Mathnawi*, I, 1-16, John Moyne; "Full Moon, Bilal," *Mathnawi*, VI, 846-952, Nicholson; "Say Who I Am," Furuzanfar number not referenced, Otto, p. 93; "Blessing the Marriage," Furuzanfar #2667, Arberry; "A Story Shams Told," Discourse #18, Arberry, "Dying," *Mathnawi*, VI, 750-776, Nicholson; "New Moon, Hilal," *Mathnawi*, VI, 1111-1215, Nicholson; untitled quatrains, Furuzanfar #553, #397, #584, #612, #496, #564, #199, #193, #194 (in the order they appear in this volume), John Moyne; "Now," Furuzanfar #644, Arberry; "The Lame Goat," *Mathnawi*, III, 1114-1127, Nicholson.

Saadi

The Gulistan, or Flower-Garden of Sa'di, tr. James Ross, Walter Scott Ltd. (London, n.d.), reprinted from the 1823 edition.

Sadi: Gulistan, or Flower-Garden, tr. James Ross, Walter Scott
Ltd (London, n.d.), reprinted from the 1823 edition.

Morals Pointed and Tales Adorned, the Bustan of Sadi, tr.
G.M.Wickens, University of Toronto Press (Toronto, 1974).

Sources for specific poems:

SAADI: "I heard of a man once...," Wickens, pp. 97-8; "A cer-
tain man, completely naked...," Ross, p. 138; "A powerful, but
moody, man...," Ross, p. 106; "A man had a beautiful wife...,"
Ross, p. 221; "They put a crow in a cage...," Ross, pp. 218-20; "I
asked a scholar...," Ross, p. 259; "A dervish's wife was preg-
nant...," Ross, p. 252-3; "Having tired of the company..., Ross,
pp. 150-1; "In Baghdad an old man...," Ross, p. 163; "The King
of Arabia heard the story...," Ross, pp. 226-8; "A certain man
entered the city...," Ross, pp. 118-9; "Whoever advises a self-
sufficient man...," Ross, p. 281; "This happened when I was
young...," Ross, p. 216-8; "One night I was thinking of what I
had done...," Ross, pp. 67-72.

Hafiz

Fifty Poems of Hafiz, tr. A.J.Arberry et al., Cambridge Univer-
sity Press (Cambridge, 1962).

E.G.Browne, *Literary History of Persia,* Cambridge University
Press (Cambridge, 1964), Vol. III.

Hafiz, *The Divan,* tr. H.Wilberforce Clarke, Octogon Press
(London, 1974), reprinted from the 1891 edition.

Michael J. Hillman, *Unity in the Ghazals of Hafiz,* Bibliotheca
Islamica (Chicago, 1976).

Sources for specific poems:

HAFIZ: "The Wild Deer," Arberry #47; "Renunciation, and
the Other Mystery," Arberry #36; "The Substance You Taste,"
Arberry #38; "Pour Me More," Arberry #42; "The Danger,"
Arberry #1; "The Zikr Circle," Clarke #243; "The Wind of an
Opening Rose," Clarke #156; "A Daughter," Clarke # 278;
"Growing Tulips," Clarke #288; "Midnight Question,"
Arberry #7; "Almost Empty," Arberry #44; "I See," Clarke
#392; "The Brim," Clarke #458; "Ruknabad," Browne, p. 291;

"Allahu Akbar Pass," Browne, p. 291; "My Response to Your Offer," Browne, p. 286; "Lost," Arberry #49; "Shiraz," Arberry #27; "Water Running Together," Arberry #24; "The Signal to Begin," Hillman, pp. 127-8; "The Banquet," Hillman, p. 112-3; "Shhh," Hillman, p. 134; "A Shift in the Breeze," Clarke #401; "That Moment in This," Arberry #14; "Taking a Riddle into the Tavern," Arberry #14; "Remember," Clarke #205; "The New Guide," Clarke #244; "Inscriptions Over the Door," Hillman, pp. 138-9; "The Wine of the Question," Hillman, p. 97; "Returning," Clarke #154.

Books of translations of Jelaluddin Rumi by Coleman
Barks:

Open Secret

Unseen Rain

We Are Three

These Branching Moments

This Longing

Delicious Laughter

Like This

Feeling the Shoulder of the Lion

One-Handed Basket Weaving

Books containing teachings of Inayat Khan include:

The Awakening of the Human Spirit

The Art of Being and Becoming

Mastery Through Accomplishment

Spiritual Dimensions of Psychology

The Music of Life

Nature Meditations

Complete Sayings

Tales

A Meditation Theme For Each Day

The Unity of Religious Ideals

Gayan

Coleman Barks is an Associate Professor of English at the University of Georgia. He has published two volumes of his own poetry: *The Juice* and *Gourd Seed*. For the last 15 years he has been collaborating with various scholars to translate the poetry of Rumi, as well as other poets. Twelve volumes have appeared from that work (beginning with *Open Secret* in 1984). The next edition of the *Norton Anthology of World Masterpieces* will include a selection of the Rumi poems.

In 1977, Coleman met the Sufi master, Bawa Muhaiyaddeen. For nine years, until Bawa's passing in 1986, he visited the Fellowship in Philadelphia several times a year. "Without that connection," Coleman says, "this work would not have ben possible for me."

Inayat Khan, founder of the Sufi Order in the West, was born in India in 1882. A master of classical Indian music by the age of twenty, he relinquished a brilliant career to devote himself to the spiritual path. In 1910, acting upon the guidance of his teacher, he became the first teacher of the Sufi tradition to come to the West. For a decade and a half he travelled throughout Europe and the United States, giving lectures and guiding an ever-growing group of seekers. In 1926, he returned to India, where he died the following year.

Information about the Sufi Order in the West may be obtained by writing to Sufi Order National Secretariat, PO Box 30065, Seattle, WA 98103.